THE P...
KN⊙⋁⋃ ME

THE PLACE THAT KNOWS ME

A Memoir

Richard Hines

Scratching Shed Publishing Ltd

Printed and bound in the UK by

Unit 600, Fareham Reach, Fareham Road
Gosport, Hampshire, PO13 0FW

For my family,
Jackie, John, Katie, Emily and Dan

'I have had some difficulties to leave the woods & heaths
& favourite spots that have known me so long...'
John Clare, rural poet, 1793-1864

Contents

Prologue

August 2013

I AM ON THE MOORS with Jackie, my wife, a few minutes' drive from our home in Sheffield. It is magnificent up here. Today the ground is purple with heather and I am cutting a few small sprigs for us to take home. On the third of September our daughter, Katie, will marry her partner, Dan, in St Ives, Cornwall. Jackie will send the sprigs we collect in two small translucent silk bags, to wish them both good luck.

It is lovely for me and her mum to see Katie so happy again. Back in the 1990s she'd had a previous long-term relationship with a member of an indie band at the same university. Later, she and he set up home together in Brighton, where the group was based. In her early twenties, she loved their music and travelling to gigs on the tour bus, particularly to the Glastonbury festival. And when they played with the now world famous The Killers, who at the time were the support act. Yet, although Katie enjoyed attending gigs being the partner of a band member didn't suit her personality. When they appeared on the BBC programme *Later... with Jools Holland* she was too self-conscious to sit among the famous musicians and their friends on the studio set and so turned down the invitation. After another gig, when the band played with The Strokes, Katie had to stop herself doing a runner when, in the dressing room, she saw Drew Barrymore, the Hollywood actor, who was a friend of the New Yorkers.

Katie's diffident nature didn't bother her partner, he was shy himself, but although they had been together for ten years things didn't work out between them in the end.

He owned the flat and, aged thirty by now, she longed for a child. Following the separation, heartbroken and alone, Katie moved to a rented one in a different area of Brighton, carrying all her worldly goods – her clothes, a few CDs and an inflatable armchair – in a taxi.

It worked out well for her when she met Dan, an ecologist.

Spending time together listening to the nightingale's song at dawn, or sitting in a meadow reading a novel while he did a survey of grasses and flowers, suited her temperament much better than Indie gigs.

DIARY ENTRY – AUGUST 2014
Emily born. 7lbs 5oz.

Tankersley Church

One

Richard with his kestrel, Kes, in 1965

1.

IT IS NOVEMBER 2015, AROUND a year after the birth of our granddaughter, when I walk – just about – on to Hove seafront. To make any progress at all, I have to lean so far forward that if the wind suddenly drops I will fall flat on my face. Waves a metre high or more crash on to the pebbly beach. In fact pebbles are piled under benches and scattered across the road. Soon, though, I have the wind at my back. A man with a dog on a lead, the only other person around, is battling into the headwind towards me. As he approaches, we grin in silent acknowledgement that the pair of us must be mad.

Ever since Emily's arrival, Jackie and I knew we wanted to be part of her life as she grew up; just as *our* children's grandparents had been part of *their* lives. We were already considering moving down here from Sheffield when, during the autumn, Katie rang to tell us that the flat next to the one she and Dan owned had come up for rent. She secured the tenancy on our behalf, Jackie now having stayed at our daughter's for the previous couple of weeks. But today, as I was pushed roughly along a now deserted seafront, doubts about our permanent relocation had crept in.

No strangers to the adjoining seaside towns of Brighton and Hove, we had visited the area often and not just to see Katie. Her older brother, John, had also chosen to live there upon leaving university fifteen years ago, he too with a degree in English Literature. We still have lovely memories of those times, among them going to Monk's House, Virginia Woolf's Sussex home, where we gazed into the garden shed in which she wrote part of her novel *To the Lighthouse*. There were trips to Charleston, the isolated farmhouse where Virginia's artist sister Vanessa Bell lived and where the Bloomsbury set were regular visitors. We dined and drank in the Bath Arms, the oldest pub in 'The Lanes', which in the nineteenth century had been Brighton's fishing quarter.

In summer we'd walked beneath cliffs where fulmars, with shallow wingbeats and glides on stiff straight wings, flew out to sea then circled back to nest ledges high on the pure white cliffs. Yet family days in fine weather are only occasional and, as the wind pushed me past rows of large and leafless elm trees, it struck me that John and Katie would be at work most days, while Emily first went to nursery and then school. Katie and Dan would want to spend their weekends together with their daughter, leaving Jackie and I on our own for an awful lot of the time. My first day here and I'd already begun to worry that we might be unsettled away from our old haunts in Yorkshire, where we have so many lifelong friends and neighbours.

Our new home was on the second floor where, that night, I was awoken by the wind rattling a window and stuffed a piece of folded paper into the loose frame while, outside in the moonlight, clouds raced across the sky. Back in my unfamiliar bed, I listened to the sea crashing on to the beach and mused over how Jackie and I, two lifelong northerners in land-bound Yorkshire, had uprooted to the Sussex coast. I couldn't rid myself of worry.

The flat was one of six in a converted late-19th century house. It had two bedrooms, one large, one small, looking on to well-kept gardens. What in its heyday would have been a splendid drawing room with a bay window, was now divided into a high-ceilinged red-tiled kitchen and white-walled living area.

By morning, yesterday's storm had been replaced by blue skies and sunshine. Lost in thought, I was sat watching the silhouettes of seagulls gliding over the tiled roofs of houses opposite when Jackie asked me to hold the tape measure. The room had two recesses, one housing an empty bookcase, the other a television. Jackie wanted to see if our large leather-topped desk, presently back in Sheffield, would fit in the first. It would. That meant we could keep it, along with a lovely chest of drawers, dated 1840, that would go nicely on the other wall with a Georgian chair circa 1780 in the window. However that was all that could be squeezed in. Every other item of furniture, accumulated over forty-six years, would either have to be sold off or given away to charity.

Soon we had a visitor, John, who walked the two miles from Brighton. 'Dad,' he said, shifting uncomfortably on a beanbag, our only form of seating currently, 'are you sure you want to abandon Yorkshire, where you have lived all your life, to come and live down here?'

'It will be nice to be near the family,' I replied.

Our daughter popped in from her flat next door. While Emily, still learning to toddle, mainly crawled around the polished wooden floorboards, Katie told us she'd asked a friend, born in Liverpool, whether she thought living next door to your parents was a little embarrassing. Her friend's answer made us laugh: 'No. It's a northern thing. All my relatives live in the same street.'

Later, with Katie wheeling Emily in a pushchair, we all walked up to a café on Richardson Road, yesterday's elm trees no longer bent double, where our granddaughter drank milk from a plastic beaker. We adults enjoyed coffee and cakes, happy to be together. Suddenly, I was convinced we'd made the right decision.

We still had plenty to sort out, like what to do with furniture and those possessions acquired over a lifetime. There was lots of unfinished business, too, that we had never got around to doing.

2.

I AM BACK IN SHEFFIELD, sitting in a blue armchair in our large Edwardian terraced house with its high ceilings, picture rails and original fireplaces. I moved here from my birthplace, Hoyland Common, at the age of thirty-six with my thirty-four-year-old wife, five-year-old son and three-year-old daughter.

A twenty-minute drive from Sheffield, Hoyland Common is a mining village five miles south of Barnsley. Jackie too was born there, as were both our children. It was also the birthplace of my parents and grandparents and Jackie's dad and his grandparents, our male ancestors drawn to the area to work in Rockingham Colliery following the sinking of a pit shaft there in 1875.

Jackie and I were married in 1970. Forty-six years living in two different houses saw us accumulate lots of stuff that must now be disposed of. Other than that desk, chest of drawers and chair destined for Hove, all of this furniture will now have to go. And we will need to decide which of our hundreds of books, photos and family items to keep hold of, all with fond memories and strong associations with our shared pasts.

Today, wedged between books on a bookshelf, I have come across a slum clearance map for Hoyland Common dated 1936.

It shows the houses to be demolished in the Queen Street area of the village. On the map, I can see the brick two-bedroomed terraced house – 2 Wroes Yard – where nineteen years earlier my mother, Annie, had been born on 20 March 1917.

Then, in a chest of drawers, I find a white apron belonging to her when she worked 'in service', aged fourteen. She would have packed this very apron in her suitcase at home the day she left Hoyland Common to begin her first job. Bought for her by her mother in Barnsley or Sheffield in 1931, it is of excellent quality. Made of heavy duty knee-length white cotton, it has strings to tie around the waist and a bib that would have been pinned to my mother's dress. In later years she still seethed with resentment at being sent into service. Leaving home, she would have told her mother that she didn't need any help and would have packed her suitcase herself. Any goodbye kiss, sign of affection or offer from her parents to see her off at the railway station, or even the bus stop, would have been rejected. Her mum and dad would have had to stand in the doorway and watch as their angry and wilful fourteen-year-old daughter strode away.

Walking out of the yard, up Queen Street, then along Sheffield Road, she would have passed the girls' school. Built of sandstone in the 1880s, this is where she had been a pupil until a couple of weeks before. Suitcase in hand, she'd have boarded the bus a little further down the road. Then, in Sheffield, she would have caught a train to Manchester to work for a family who had a shop near the docks. One day, a large group of sailors came in, laughing and shouting, crowding around, teasing her, picking up things off the counter and shelves. Frightened, she ran out and into a nearby shop and asked for help. That shopkeeper asked the men to buy something or leave and stayed with her until they had gone. My mother's other duties involved cooking and cleaning the house. She had a half-day off each week, which didn't give her time to catch the train home and back. It was six months before she returned to Hoyland Common having been given her first holiday. The first weeks away from home were awful, she once told me. Every night she would cry herself to sleep in bed in her attic room, until her heart hardened and she grew more used to her new life.

Later on, she moved to a job in Southport on the Lancashire coast to work for a woman with a small child. This time she was treated more like a friend than a servant and on fine afternoons they would stroll together down fashionable Lord Street to meet up for tea and cakes with her employer's friends, who included her in their conversations.

In contrast to her Southport employer, when she next moved to a job in Sheffield her new employer treated her with little respect. She met my dad when she was eighteen, so it would have been 1935 when he cycled over from Hoyland Common to see her. He hadn't known servants' visitors weren't allowed to go to the front door and was curtly sent to the back. Mother overheard her employers mocking his working-class Barnsley accent.

By coincidence, after dad left that day, Mabel, a friend from Hoyland Common also in service nearby, called in for a visit and found my mother stamping around in the kitchen and banging cutlery, plates and pans down onto the worktops as she prepared dinner. Still infuriated by how my dad had been treated, she told Mabel what had gone on. Concerned Mother's employers would overhear her ranting, Mabel held a finger to her lips and told her to shush. Saying she didn't care if they did, she banged another pan on a worktop and knocked over a colander of peas. In the end, the two nineteen-year-old girls ended up on their knees, laughing together as they picked the peas off the kitchen floor.

One summer evening earlier that year, back home in Hoyland Common on their days off, my mother and Mabel had walked to a fair in Elsecar, a nearby mining village, where two young men, one destined to become my dad, began talking to them. The four got on well, walking around the stalls and going on the rides. Ironically, though, it was the other young man who walked

Richard with his mother, dad and older Barry (in black trunks) in Blackpool

Mother home. She never told me how their courtship began. Presumably they began to see each other around the village and would stop to talk. However it started, they hit it off. My dad had been put off drink by his alcoholic grandad and heavy drinking dad and didn't go in pubs. Working-class girls in mining villages didn't drink alcohol back then either. So, as both of them were film fans, their first date would have most likely been a visit to the Kino, our local cinema. Then, out of the blue, a few months after they met, their relationship was thrown into doubt. Dad had seven siblings, a younger brother and six sisters, and his dad decided to leave Hoyland Common and move to Bradford, so the girls could find work at Lister's mill in Manningham. He was nearly twenty-five at the time, but having nowhere to live in the village he had no choice but to go with his family.

Dad couldn't settle in Bradford. He saw it as a dull mill town where he had no personal history; no fond memories; no happy associations. He told me how he worked for a demolition firm and missed the camaraderie of fellow miners he'd known since being a boy. Oh, how he hated where he lived, in the shadow of the mill; streets and streets of terraced houses going on for miles. He missed the woods, the flower meadows and golden wheat fields that surrounded Hoyland Common, only minutes' walk in any direction. Most of all he missed the lass who became my mother. So, after six months in Bradford he returned to his roots.

Soon, he got his old job at Rockingham Colliery back and lodged with his Auntie Lena, a widow whose husband had been killed in the pit. To supplement her meagre pension she also had another lodger, also a miner, now retired. Dad amused me when he spoke of this man's end-of-day ritual. Sitting in an armchair in the living room, he'd open the doors of a cupboard, put his feet up on a shelf, light a cigarette, and say, 'I'll have a cig, then go to bed.' Many years later, Auntie Lena bought Jackie and me the sweetest, most touching wedding present. The day before we married I answered a knock on the door to find her, now well into her eighties, standing there in a long black coat. After having apologised for not being able to afford a proper present, she said she was sure we would find these useful, and handed me a bucket and scrubbing brush.

Dad enjoyed being her lodger. She was kind and from her house in Sale Street he could hear the skylarks singing in the fields each summer and the swifts screeching as they flew up to their nests in the eaves of her house and others in the street.

Soon after he returned from Bradford he and Mother were engaged. They had planned to marry in a few months' time but her dad, believing she was too young at eighteen to come to such a decision, refused to give her permission until she was twenty-one. As things turned out, they married on the first Saturday after 20 March 1938, the day of her twenty-first birthday. Knowing her, it would have been she who did all the organising.

I was eighteen when my beloved dad died in 1963 and, although heartbroken, nothing had been left unresolved. Over the years – even now – every autumn I feel a sense of loss; the same sweet sad yearning that had been stirred in me by a robin's song on that September day when the grass glistened with dew and dad's coffin was lowered into the earth. Although he died over half a century ago, I still have one of the very shovels he used down the mine that he brought home after getting a new one. I've fetched it up from the cellar and dusted off the cobwebs. Picking it up with the smooth wooden handle, my left hand is holding it in the very place his hand would have gripped as he shovelled the shining black coal.

I recall how, in the early 1950s, he and Mother liked ballroom dancing. They also enjoyed visiting London. Each autumn they left me to stay with my grandma, and although we didn't have a car, they went to the Motor Show in Earl's Court on a jaunt organised by a local pub landlord, who drove the coach. The trip also included a couple of nights in a hotel and seeing the sights; the Tower of London, Petticoat Lane market and Oxford Street, where they called in at Harrods to buy me lovely presents. One year it was a replica-size Colt 45 pistol, like the ones used in the cowboy films I watched at the Kino. Another year they bought me a boys' size longbow, with arrows that had real feather flights.

Dad was a kind, gentle, easy-going man. Mother was stricter and more confident. She would go up to school for parents' evenings. If my brother Barry or I had a problem at school, it was she who went to see the head teacher. The thought of talking to a schoolteacher intimidated Dad, yet deep underground, his helmet lamp throwing shadows on the pitch black tunnel walls, he shovelled sixteen tons of coal every day. And although this shovel is the only direct touchable connection I have to him and his mining history, we have nowhere to keep it in Hove.

So, unlike Mother's apron, his shovel, although equally dear to me, will end up on the council dump.

3.

I KEEP NATURE DIARIES ON my computer and record any wildlife I see. Tankersley is a ten-minute walk from Hoyland Common through countryside and I drive over there regularly from Sheffield. Today in my documents file I noticed one entitled 'Skylark's Song'. When I clicked on it, it turned out the diary I'd kept in 1994 wasn't just about an encounter with a wild creature.

17 March 1994
Tankersley. A skylark sings. A strong smell of earth. Looking over his shoulder in his tractor cab, the farmer watched the dark soil peel off the plough blade. A weasel ran across the lane opposite the church. I went to look for it and saw its tiny pointed face looking up from the hedge bottom. For a moment our eyes met before going about our separate lives. Its, in damp grass and dark tunnels. A life of immediacy. Of overpowering smells and racing blood. Of squeals and struggles and death. Mine. A life of reflection and anger.

Reading that has dredged up things from my past which still hurt. My brother Barry, six years older, was a successful writer. His novel, *A Kestrel for A Knave*, published in 1968, sold well over a million copies and was the following year made into the film *Kes,* directed by Ken Loach. Since 1999, the book has been a Penguin Modern Classic. So I was used to being over-shadowed, but coming second to him in our mother's affections upset me. As I sat on that churchyard bench after seeing the weasel, my mind had begun to dwell on Mother's death the previous August when, on a beautiful late-summer's night, a large full moon had been visible through the hospital window. Moments before she lost consciousness, never to speak again, her last words were: 'I'll miss Richard'. Then, 'I'll miss Barry.' I was surprised at how pleased I felt because Mother had said my name before his.

My thoughts then jumped to her funeral. After my beloved dad's, nothing was left unsaid, no questions went unanswered. On that September day when the grass glistened with dew as his coffin was lowered into the earth, the robin's song had caught the sad sweet yearning I'd felt at his loss. I had no such feelings after Mother's burial. Just hurt and animosity.

After the service at St Peter's Church and laying to rest in Kirk Balk Cemetery, Barry and I went to see a life-long friend of Mother's and neighbour from our childhood who'd been too ill to attend. We'd only just seen Mother into her grave but that didn't prevent this old woman from making a heartbreaking revelation. Mother, she said, had once told her that Barry was everything to her, the most important thing in her life.

On the previous day in the Chapel of Rest, I'd been unable to bring myself to leave. I'd take a last look at her, close the door, then repeatedly go back for another, unable to bear the thought that she was gone forever. Now, when the family went to visit the grave and admire the flowers and tributes of respect, I stood in sullen silence. Betrayed. I felt no tenderness or pity, only a selfish impotent rage at not being able to confront her about what her friend had said. But it was too late now. Her chance to reflect ... to explain ... to reassure ... had gone forever.

Those old wounds had also been unearthed recently when,

one evening in The Prince of Wales pub in Hoyland Common, a woman who had moved away from the village years ago and was visiting friends approached me. She told me how when she was nine or ten years old, at my mother's request, she would regularly call at our house to take me for a walk around the village in my pram and then added, laughing, that I was 'mardy', always crying as a baby. Maybe she was pleasanter when a girl. Although I can't fully recall her appearance, I do remember thinking her awfully hard-faced. I ended up arguing

Richard's mother, Annie

with her when she called a lad we had both known 'a queer' and 'a poof' because he' liked dancing. I wouldn't have allowed her to take our dog for a walk, never mind let her take one of our children out in a pram.

Hurtful memories still trouble me. On my first day in infant school in September 1950, my mother didn't take me there, an older girl did. She left me just inside the classroom door, while the other five year-old boys and girls stood with their mothers. The only father there held his screaming son's hand as he pulled him into the classroom. Once inside, the boy pulled his hand free from his dad's, took something out of his own mouth and threw it. When it hit the window it stuck; I could see it was a piece of red-and-white-striped seaside rock.

I can also remember being in hospital when I was three or four years old, having my tonsils out. From my cot at night, in the reflection of the ward's large windows, I could see other cots and nurses dressed in white. I asked for a drink. The water was warm, it tasted awful. Soon after the nurse left I felt sick. Fearing I'd be in trouble, I lifted the pillow, vomited, and then placed the pillow over the sick before laying my head on it.

The next image I recall from that time must have happened earlier that day – walking down a long hospital corridor holding a woman's hand I'd looked up, expecting to see my mother. But it wasn't her. It was Mrs Ibbotson, who lived a few doors up from us in Tinker Lane.

One later time I was seven or eight years old, when my parents wouldn't have left me in the house alone, so Barry must have been around somewhere. But I was definitely by myself when Dad returned from visiting friends and gently broke the news that my mother had been taken ill and wouldn't be coming home that night. To which I'd replied: 'Good.' Furious, he told me off.

Now, over sixty years later, I began to wonder whether her neglect of me as a child was rooted in something more complex, an idea that set me off searching through a box of black and white family photographs. One I remembered of her and a large group of women standing in front of a formidable Victorian building had gone missing. But I did find another photo and have it here in front of me now, on the table.

Around fifty women are lined up in four rows in what appears to be the grounds of a hospital. The back two rows are standing, the second row seated on chairs, the front row sitting on a lawn with a floral border. All are wearing dresses and cardigans in the styles of the 1940s or early-1950s. There are two exceptions: the matron in her white uniform and another uniformed nurse. Next to the end of the third row is my mother who, despite a wan smile on her face, looks worn out. Was this some sort of convalescent home? I can't be sure, but I guess my mother had been referred there by Dr Marie Allott, our village doctor, because, as Mother used to put it, she suffered from 'nerves'.

Once, when I was seven or eight years old, she looked at me with one eye almost closed and asked if I thought she looked ill. She looked alright to me, except for the temporary squint, and I couldn't see how that showed she was poorly. I thought she was 'putting it on'. Of course, I'd never heard of nervous breakdowns, anxiety or depression. She was a poor sleeper, I do know that, who later became addicted to sleeping pills the doctor prescribed. Perhaps she hadn't started taking them yet in my younger years, but from the time I was old enough to get myself ready for school she would be zonked out, unable to get out of bed.

Years later, when she had given them up, she told me how she still occasionally woke in the night and lay in the dark, overcome with fear and anxiety.

I see now that her apparent neglect of me could have been down to illness. Maybe she had been in the hospital/convalescent home when I went into hospital and my dad, who worked on the morning shift, had arranged for Mrs Ibbotson to take me in? And perhaps she had been ill on the day I started school and Dad had arranged for an older girl to make sure I got there safely.

On one occasion, when she was in her sixties, I called in to see her and she told me how, following my birth, she'd suffered from mastitis. Her breasts became so infected they turned black and blue, so painful she couldn't breast feed me. And I wonder if that is why she couldn't bond with and feel fond of me.

After my wife, Jackie, read my diary and rants, she reminded me how I used to ring my mother several times a week, and that she could hear us talking and laughing together.

When Jackie put that photo from the hospital/convalescent home back in the box, she took another one out. In it, I am sitting in a field of buttercups with Mother and both of us are smiling.

4.

WHEN MOTHER MARRIED DAD IN 1938, their first home in Hoyland Common was a rented brick terraced house in New Street. Until one winter's day the local rag and bone man loaded their furniture on to his cart and, in deep snow, led his horse along New Street, Central Street and Queen Street to a rented low-ceilinged stone cottage in Tinker Lane. In 1955, when I was ten and Barry sixteen, the two of them bought a late nineteenth-century semi-detached house a little further up the road. With Dad leading the way, Barry and me helped to carry our furniture the twenty yards or so up to number 56.

Having not been on Tinker Lane for years, I parked the car outside that second house recently. From the outside, it looked much as it did when my parents bought it seventy-odd years ago. Mother and Dad modernised the back downstairs room, which thereafter served as a kitchen/dining room. Aged ten when we moved in, I hated it. It had a large black kitchen range and stone sink and, by the pantry door, a patch of shiny brown oilcloth was pasted on to flowered wallpaper. Mother told me this was where Mr Wilkinson, a one-legged man who'd lived in the house before us, leaned his crutch. The image of such a man in this very space scared me. Dad told me not to be silly. He explained that Mr Wilkinson had lost his leg fighting in the First World War, and how when he'd returned home he became a cobbler. The large shed in the garden beside the house, with its window facing on to the road, had been his shop. Knowing Mother, I'd guess it was her idea to rent it out at two shillings and sixpence a week. Soon there was a sign above it: 'Bernard Vickers. General Dealer'. Unkempt, probably in his fifties but looking older and wearing a long dark overcoat, Bernard would shuffle up Tinker Lane with a wicker basket on one arm, laden with supplies to sell ... tinned food ... sliced bread ... soft drinks ... sweets ... all of it bought from Scarrot's Warehouse in Regent Street.

Barry was studying for his 'O' levels at the time and we both found Bernard amusing. His shop had no water supply and twice a day he'd bring an empty jug to be filled with water so he could make more tea. Standing just inside the back door he'd hum to himself, while we glanced at each other and tried not to laugh as we waited for Mother to hand it back full. It was then that we'd hear him say his trademark 'thank-YOU', which started as a whisper and ended almost as a shout.

Charlie Whitworth, who wore a black flat cap and had a leather strap coiled around his wrist to strengthen it after a mining accident, was a friend of Bernard's. If Charlie hadn't time to call in for a chat, when he walked past he'd ask after his health by calling, 'Alright, Bernard?' But their friendship ended one day when Charlie threw a brick through the shop window after learning that his wife, Little Marion, and Bernard had been having an affair. Poor old Charlie was so upset he went to bed and refused to get up. Two days later, his wife called the police and they came to the house and ordered him to get out of bed.

Bernard's shop was a magnet for the village 'characters' and eccentrics. The most well-known of these was Stan Waddy. One story claimed Stan's fame was worldwide, relating how when he'd travelled to Rome and stood on the balcony in St Peter's Square with the Pope, people in the crowds below had asked: 'Who's that bloke with Stan?' According to Hoyland Common folklore, as a young man he had sold fruit and vegetables from a cart pulled by a donkey. When I knew him he was middle-aged, unshaven, scruffily dressed and known for outrageous lies. One day in July, at the time of Hoyland Common Fair, he marched into the taproom of the Cross Keys and shouted: 'I need six men to collect a helter-skelter from Retford.' Another time, empty wicker basket on his arm, he insisted he'd sold out of crabs caught earlier that day by himself in Clacton-on-Sea, two hundred and forty miles away. Once, he told me he'd been mushrooming and had found a mushroom so big that when he'd pulled it up there was a sheep underneath it, fast asleep.

I'd never given a thought to *why* he told such whopping lies, or what life would be like for his wife and two daughters, until one day I came out of our garden gate and saw his thin, poverty-stricken missus hanging on to his coat as he tried to escape her. She wouldn't let go her grip and so off he walked, dragging her behind him, while she clung on begging money to buy food. In the end he stopped, put a hand in his pocket, brought a handful of coins out, showed them to his wife on an open palm and said: 'Look. It's all I've got and Jesus Christ couldn't take that off me.'

His poor defeated wife gave up and walked back up the lane, in the direction of home, sobbing.

I am now on the pavement in front of where 62 Tinker Lane once stood, the house I lived in for the first ten years of my life. The row of four stone cottages to which it belonged, 60 to 66, have since been demolished, their foundations buried under the large garden of a modern bungalow. The Lamberts lived at number 60. Every morning, Mrs Lambert would step out into the lane and shake her duster as she sang along to *Housewives' Choice*, a record request show on BBC radio's Light Programme.

The Jones's lived at 64. Mr Jones, who had black combed-back hair, worked the night shift and slept in the day. On one occasion when I was little, riding my bike on the pavement, I disturbed his sleep. He jumped out of bed and knocked so hard on his window he broke the glass and had to go buy a pane to re-glaze it.

Miss Sylvester was at number 66. A very old woman, born in the reign of Queen Victoria, she wore black ankle-length dresses and black ankle-boots, which fastened with buttons. She baked her own bread and often asked me to go to the shop to buy her a small quantity of barm – yeast – to make the bread rise. When I returned from the errand she'd slip a coin in my hand. Each time I hoped it might be more, but was disappointed when I saw the usual tuppence on my open palm.

I recall tin baths in front of a blazing fire and how, from my bedroom, the mournful sound of the Rockingham Colliery siren could be heard calling the 6.00am 'day' shift in to work, soon to be followed by the clattering of a torrent of miners' clogs.

It was considered bad luck by some to work on Good Friday, so they stayed home. My paternal grandad, a conscientious man who flew two racing pigeons, one called Semolina, the other Something Hot, and who wore a pink dog rose in his lapel, had nevertheless gone to work on Good Friday 1946. The sound of clogs tramping up Tinker Lane mid-shift thereafter would have caused a wave of anxiety through the village. Fathers, mothers, wives, daughters, sons, sisters and brothers of those who had gone in would have stepped out from house and shop doorways. Men would have looked up from their digging in allotments. Or emerged from their pigeon loft. Anxious enquiries would have been answered with calls of: 'Doug Westerman's been killed,' carrying the news along the village streets and to farmers in the fields. I was only ten months old. Barry, seven, was playing in the prefabricated bungalows being built back then in Tinker Lane when he heard the shouts. Only knowing him as Grandad, he hadn't realised it was our mother's father they were talking about. Until, that is, he returned home and saw Mother crying and our dad standing awkwardly beside her.

Richard and Barry in a garden near their Tinker Lane cottage, post-World War Two

It was a roof fall that did it. Years later, when I was eight or nine years old, Mother told me that when my uncle Eddie, her brother, had gone to identify his dad's body he'd seen how a chain had somehow fallen across his face and left an imprint of links on his skin. That image scared me. Even so, if another boy talked gleefully of a ghastly accident he'd heard about, I'd shamelessly use my tale to top his by saying, 'That's nowt. When my grandad got killed he had a chain imprinted across his face.'

Topping each other's grisly stories is what we boys did and I don't feel bad about it. But standing on the pavement in front of where 62 Tinker Lane once stood has unearthed a memory of something I did while living there that I do still feel guilty about.

Each Christmas holiday, with dad carrying a suitcase, our family would walk up Queen Street to Sheffield Road and catch the bus to Bradford for a family gathering at my grandparents' house in Manningham. My dad's sister, Auntie Hannah, had a congenital disease which caused irregular growth of the head and affected the shape of her face. Her eyes seemed too near to the edge of her out-of-shape skull; too far apart. And the little round glasses she wore had to have a really long piece across her nose.

As a child, she'd rarely attended school and couldn't read. She once told me her biggest problem with that was how when she stood at a bus stop she couldn't read the destination on the front of the bus, so didn't know where it was going.

The family laughed affectionately when we played cards with Auntie Hannah. She was confused by the rules of the game and sat next to Auntie Kath, who played her hand for her. When anyone else won, they left their winnings of a few coppers on the table in front of them. But when she won, she would scrape the kitty of pennies from the centre of the table, unclip her handbag, take out her purse, pour the coppers into it, then put the purse back into her handbag and clip it shut again. One Christmas she made us laugh when she said a woman had wished her a Merry Christmas, and that she'd told her 'I've enough on my plate.'

At one Christmas family gathering in Bradford, I would have been nine or ten years old at the time, I witnessed one scene that stays with me.

Self-conscious about her looks and old-fashioned clothes, Auntie Hannah cried as she told her mother she didn't want to go to the party at Lister's wool mill, where she worked. My grandma insisted she must, pushed her out of the house and closed the door. A couple of hours later, she returned home. She was tipsy and laughed excitedly as she told us Mr Peter, one of the managers, had kissed her on the cheek and danced with her. Then, smiling dreamily, she did a couple of whirls, reliving her dance with her boss, probably the happiest moment of her life.

I was fond of Auntie Hannah and was moved to see her return so happy, but that didn't stop me betraying her when, along with our other Bradford relatives, she came to stay at Auntie Kath's the following summer. She asked me to walk down to our house with her and I was overcome with dread. Back then, in the 1950s, attitudes to disabled people were awful. I feared we might be mocked from behind the cupped hands of sniggering youths. To my relief there were no kids about in the first couple of streets, but when we reached Central Street I decided to take a short cut across overgrown land where houses had been demolished and Auntie Hannah followed. 'You can't come this way,' I told her. 'There's a high wall to climb over. You'll have to go the long way round.'

She looked at me from under the beret pulled low over her misshapen forehead. And under her little round glasses, her wide -apart eyes filled with tears. She knew I was ashamed to be seen with her. For a moment I was going to turn back and walk beside her after all, but my embarrassment got the better of me. Striding over stones and bricks from the demolition, instead I ran through the grass and weeds, climbed over the wall into a backyard and then up an entry into Tinker Lane, leaving poor Auntie Hannah to find her own way home.

Today, as I stand on the pavement outside, my mind also digs out the ghost of a tragedy that happened on this very spot over sixty years ago. In 1949 or 1950, when we were four or five years old, my friend Brian Utley and I were playing on our little three-wheeler bikes outside our house. Back then, hardly anyone in the village had a car and so the lane was traffic free, except for the occasional greengrocer's or butcher's van delivering orders to people's doors. I don't know if this particular greengrocer was delivering to our house or a neighbour's, but Brian climbed off his bike and crawled underneath the parked van. He was still beneath it when the fellow, having delivered the order, climbed back into the cab and drove off oblivious.

I have no personal memory of the actual events of that day. And I'd have never even known about my childhood friend, had Mother not decided to tell me what had happened to him years later. She cried as she told how, on hearing the news, Brian's mother, Mrs Utley, had rushed to the scene, picked up her son in her arms and carried him up Queen Street and along Sheffield Road, leaving a trail of blood all the way to Dr Allott's surgery.

But it was too late. Poor Brian was already dead.

5.

HAVING WALKED FIFTY YARDS FURTHER down Tinker Lane, I am now at the top of a cart track. From here, I can see the spire of St Peter's Church at the top of Law Hill, about a mile away. Stretching out before it are large monotonous fields of dull green rye grass, enclosed by an occasional hawthorn hedge.

Today the weather is overcast and grey, but had it been bright and sunny this landscape would still be a depressing sight to people of my generation, and the generations of my parents and grandparents who lived in the village. All would have memories of a time when those meadows of white ox-eye daises, buttercups and purple vetch had skylarks singing high overhead. I recall a male linnet on a tall bending stalk of grass and marvelling at the crimson patches either side of his breast feathers. And how grey partridge would shoot up from under my feet and whirr away on swept-back wings, startling me and making my heart race.

The country names of birds had passed down the generations and we boys still used them. We'd watch 'Jenny Wrens' flitting around in the undergrowth. Or crouch over a low bush or bank, to peer in at the dark scribbles on the white eggs in the nest of a 'Scribble Lark' – a yellowhammer.

When I was a lad, the narrow rutted path on which I stand was called the 'Mush'. I don't know why. Maybe in the past those fields it leads to were a good place to collect mushrooms and the name is an abbreviation of mushroom fields. I haven't set foot here for many years. In the hedge on the left, house sparrows are chittering, as they always have. Beyond it are the derelict buildings of what we called Lawton's farm – market garden really – where the greengrocer grew the vegetables to sell in his two family shops on Hoyland Common. All that's left of the farm now is a half-collapsed large ugly corrugated shed which used to be guarded by Blackie, a dog who reared up at the end of a chain, barking crazily every time I passed by with my mates.

On the right of the cart track are the same detached concrete garages as were there back then, but no longer in use. Long grass and weeds have grown in front of their double doors. Sometimes, on my way to the fields, I'd walk down the track although mostly behind the garages and along a path through the allotments. One of them had a pig sty and I used to love to clamber up and reach in to touch their bristly pink backs. In the mornings, it would be miners on afternoon shift on their allotments, in an afternoon the men working early morning day or night shifts. I'd see them digging and turning over soil with their spades. On my morning walks, second best after stroking grunting pigs was watching the flocks of racing pigeons flying above while the miners rattled tins of peas to call them down to their lofts before work.

I am surprised to discover that nowadays this path has a gate. I unlatch it and walk through. What I expect to see ... rows of vegetables ... runner beans climbing up garden canes ... large metal watering cans ... and what I hope to hear ... the cooing of pigeons in lofts ... are absent. Today, this land has paddocks of geese and ducks and is home to grazing horses.

Unable to get to the fields, I turn back. On spare land behind the garages a man wearing blue overalls has his head under a car bonnet. I ask if he knows what had happened to the allotments.

The Hines family in Scarborough, 1957, Barry in his Teddy Boy suit.

Standing up and wiping his greasy hands on a cloth, he says he'd heard the bloke who turned it into a smallholding either bought or now rents the land from the council. I don't know whether it's my accent or if he has a vague memory of seeing me in the village but he asks if I am a Hoyland Commoner. It turns out that not only are we both natives, we've both lived in Tinker Lane, him at 82 and me at 62 and 56. He then says something that strikes my heart with a pang of regret, reminding me that Jackie and I will soon have upped-sticks and moved to Hove. He tells me he spent many years in different countries and parts of Britain serving in the Army, but that on being demobbed there was only one place he wished to live: Hoyland Common, his home village.

If someone had blindfolded me and led me to the bottom of this track, before removing it and letting me see, I'd still have no idea where I am. Having walked down it with eyes open, I see a half-submerged sofa in what used to be a clear stream, its banks overgrown with brambles and goose grass. A car radiator sticks out of the green algae that covers its now-stagnant surface.

The lower part of what used to be a flower meadow is also overgrown – with silver birch and willow trees – and as I walk between trunks and duck under branches I struggle to find my bearings. I had thought I was standing where a concrete bridge had once been. In the winter of 1962-63, the first snow fell just after Christmas and didn't thaw until March. I'd sledge down the meadow and across it. Dad was in bed with what turned out to be terminal cancer and on one occasion, when I told him I'd seen ten-foot snowdrifts, he said, 'I wish I'd been well enough to come with you, lad.' Today, I see no bridge, so disorientated that I can't be sure this is where it was. I walk on to see if it's further along.

The thing must have been demolished. Had it still existed, I'd surely have walked past it by now. The water running under it flowed into a pond we called 'The Floods'. When I was aged six or seven, the Second World War with Germany was a very recent memory. Lads at that time, including me, would find large stones and pieces of wood to heave into the pond. When they hit the water with an enormous splash we'd shout 'Bombs over Berlin!' A sweeter and more palatable memory is how I once discovered a moorhen's nest in the reeds at the edge of The Floods, and stood mesmerised as a chick pecked its way out of its eggshell. All these years on, The Floods too seem to have vanished.

After walking on between birch and willow, I find myself next to a small lake that has chest-high reeds. I wonder if, over the years, the reeds I found in the moorhens' nest have grown chest-high. Perhaps this is the place I'm looking for. But then I emerge from the trees onto rough grass and see a dual-carriageway.

My memories of this landscape don't contrast happily with traffic and I feel strangely bereft, as if I've lost contact with my own history. I walk back to where I thought the concrete bridge had been, jump across the stream and try to scramble up the steep grassy bank between brambles. But my boots repeatedly slip and I keep sliding back down. Eventually, the knees of my jeans covered in mud, I grab the slim silver trunk of a sapling birch and manage to hoist myself up. Across a field, at the bottom of Tinker Lane, I spot a row of prefabricated houses, surrounded now by a redbrick outer wall. One in particular at last helps me to work out where I am. When I was young, a path used to run beside the end prefab and down to the concrete bridge. From here, I see I'd been yards to the left of where it crossed the stream.

I jump back across. Looking through the trees in the direction I'd walked earlier I now have no trouble remembering what this view was like back then. The bridge was about thirty yards along from where I now stand and the stream flowing under it into The Floods some fifty yards downstream. Dominating the landscape beyond – and visible for miles – Rockingham Colliery slag heap once loomed, dumper truck on its way to the top to tip another dusty load. I can now work out that, earlier, I'd been walking on the now-levelled land the slag heap stood on for over a century. And that small lake with the chest-high reeds had once been the newt pond beside the railway line that ran through the pit yard – where all those cars, heavy goods vehicles and buses nowadays tear noisily through the landscape.

One of my best friends at junior school was Budgie, a small stocky lad with sandy hair. I gave him the nickname because we saw an escaped budgerigar on the colliery slag heap once and he chased it until it landed, too tired to fly any longer. Then he picked it up and carefully carried it home.

Now, walking along the stream, I pass a large ash tree. Over sixty years ago, Budgie and I were on this track when four men ran towards us shouting: 'Get out of the way! Horse loose!' Scared, we clambered up this very tree and sat perched on high. Moments later came the sound of galloping hooves. We watched it canter under our branch while the men stood across the track waving their arms above their heads, shouting: 'Whoa!' But the horse didn't stop, Budgie and me, safe in the tree, couldn't stop laughing as they either ran or jumped into the stream to get out of its way.

Walking back to the car now, I smiled as I thought of other such antics Budgie and I – and other lads – got up to. The colliery was a brilliant place to play.

Steam trains pulling wagons of coal into the pit yard passed beneath a footbridge and sent up great billows of smoke through the gaps in the planks. We, meanwhile, would disappear into the smoke, whooping with delight. After pushing it to get it going, Budgie, myself and a couple of other lads once jumped onto a flat-topped trolley used by workmen to check the railway lines. As it gained speed down an incline, we hurtled through the yard past men the working there, who yelled at us to get off.

As the year progressed, we would walk down Tinker Lane and along a path to see the Shetland pit ponies. They spent the year underground, living in stables between their two daily eight-hour shifts. During the colliery's annual summer holiday they were brought to the surface and we would watch them nibbling grass or running around the field, kicking their back legs into the air.

I was told that my paternal great grandad Hines left working the land in Lincolnshire to work on the railways. He ended up driving a shunting engine, hauling coal along the many railway tracks in the pit yard.

Mr Ullyott, who had a farm a few hundred yards up the lane from the colliery, also worked there and his team of Shire horses hauled railway wagons full of coal around the pit yard. I once saw him, looking strikingly small beside them, leading his horses to the colliery. A beautiful white one was playing up, throwing back its head and veering off to the side of the lane. Months later, I heard Mr Ullyott had been killed, accidently crushed to death by one of his horses. The memory of him leaning into the massive white one's shoulder, grimly holding onto its reins as he struggled to keep it walking straight, has stayed with me.

6.

ON MY WAY BACK TO the car in Tinker Lane, I stopped to take in the view of the fields that lead up to St Peter's Church at the top of Law Hill. An earlier building, Hoyland Chapel, had once stood on a site where, at some point in the seventeenth or eighteenth century, a notice announcing that these fields would henceforth be 'enclosed' had been nailed to the door – the date, presumably, when the hedgerows I knew as a lad were planted. I had always intended looking up the exact details sometime, but our imminent move to Hove prompted me to do so now.

Back home in Sheffield, I dug out a book by Arthur Clayton that I was sure would contain the information. Arthur was a hundred and one years old when he died in 2002. The inscription on his gravestone (which is near my parent's grave) reads: 'A local historian. A true gentleman. Loved by many.'

I was certainly fond of him. Arthur worked at Rockingham Colliery at the same time as Dad and I'd often stop to talk to him on my walks around the village. His book has yellow cardboard covers, held together by a black sticky-tape spine. Typed on a manual typewriter, photocopied and stapled together, it is the ugliest and most unprofessional looking publication among my and Jackie's books. Yet it is one of our most treasured. Entitled *Hoyland*, it is a fascinating history of the small township and surrounding areas, including Hoyland Common.

Arthur wrote that the fields to be enclosed were common land on Earl Fitzwilliam's Wentworth Estate and that the earl, like many wealthy landowners, wanted to 'improve' said open fields and wastelands by turning them into more 'productive' arable and mixed farmland. And so we learn that, on 17 February 1794, Earl Fitzwilliam presented a petition to the House of Commons 'praying' for a Bill to be passed to enclose and divide the open fields, commons, and waste grounds of Hoyland.

For centuries, the tenants who farmed the Wentworth Estate paid the earl 'money rent'. They also paid him 'boon rent', which meant working a number of days for the earl on his estate or supplying him with teams of horses or oxen to plough its fields. And on top of this, there was something called 'fowls rent', which meant they were further obligated to provide a number of hens or capons for the earl's table in the big house.

The tenant farmers worked to an open or three-field system; a medieval method wherein fields had long narrow strips of ploughed soil known as 'lands', between which were unploughed divisions called 'baulks'. In writing his book, Arthur specifically researched the common over the road from Hoyland Chapel and found written evidence that it had contained one hundred and sixty-eight lands and nine baulks. Eighteenth century ploughs had large wheels, the better to navigate heavy clay soil when pulled by oxen and horses. They were awkward to turn around however, so cultivating long strips with no hedges or fences and turning on a 'headland' at the end of the field was most efficient. Crops of wheat, barley and oats were planted in a two or three-year rotation and a third field left fallow, which allowed nutrients to return to soil grazed by the village herds. The earl's tenants' livestock – oxen, cows, horses – also fed on hay from communal meadows. Over many centuries, tenants on aristocratic estates

East front of Wentworth Woodhouse – as painted by Allan Womsley.

had such 'rights of common', which allowed them not only to farm on the commons, but also to fish in the streams and gather berries, firewood and the timber they used for building from the woods.

Imagine their lives as they worked that land in early spring, larks singing overhead while they walked behind their plough, the smell of fresh earth as it peeled smoothly off the blade. At planting time, these fields would be busy with farmers scattering handfuls of seed into every freshly-driven furrow.

By June, the knee-high wheat would be turning golden. On the edges of the long fields beside the baulks, purple vetch, blue forget-me-nots and tiny bluebird's eye speedwell would be in flower. The communal hay meadows would be a pinkish haze of grasses set off by bright yellow buttercups and tall white ox-eye daisies. Then, on one of those long summer days when the weather was fine, haymaking would commence and the rhythmic swing of the farmers' scythes would fell those grasses and flowers. Whole families would carry and pitchfork the hay on to horse-drawn carts. And, when it had all been piled high, the children would clamber on top and ride to the communal barn where the hay was stored to feed the animals over winter.

In late summer and early autumn, the swishing scythe blades would send these golden crops of wheat and barley toppling. Working all day and taking advantage of the harvest moon, men, women and older children would scoop up armfuls with which to make 'stooks'; sheaves of grain stood upright on the fields of stubble. On the flat floor of a barn, men using flails would thrash wheat and barley. Women would do the winnowing; throwing grain into the air to separate the wheat or barley from the chaff.

Working the common land together; gathering in the hay and harvest together. In autumn, collecting acorns to feed the pigs together; in winter, gathering firewood together.

Rural Hoyland would have had a sense of being in tune with nature. A family feeling of belonging, fostered by a connection to ancestors who had worked this common for centuries. Until, on 17 April 1794, two months to the day since the House of Commons had been petitioned by Earl Fitzwilliam, Royal Assent was granted with the skylarks still singing overhead.

That notice nailed on the Hoyland Chapel door announced that the earl was about to 'quick' – plant hedges of quickthorn or hawthorn – to enclose the common land. No longer would folk be able to farm their communal plots of land, having lost their 'rights of common'. What fear, despair and desperation these Hoyland families must have felt as they crowded around and listened to someone who could read delivering the news that their livelihoods had just been stolen by one of the richest men in the country.

7.

ST PETER'S CHURCH SPIRE is visible for miles. In 1955, aged ten, I attended its Sunday school. Fieldy, a couple of years older than me, lived in Tinker Lane and would call for me on the way. As we walked along he would grin knowingly and tell me about divorce cases he'd read of in that morning's *News of the World*, where husbands or wives had been unfaithful or 'intimate with a lover'. I didn't know what he was on about.

Swearing was not allowed in our house, not even bloody. Mother or Dad might say 'damn' or 'blast', but only if things got really bad. Any bad language in the presence of my parents embarrassed me. I loved poetry and stole an anthology from school once, but when I got it home I discovered a fellow pupil had written 'FUCK' in blue ink on the flyleaf. When Mother and Dad were out, I emptied the black ink from my fountain pen, filled it with blue ink and got to work. I joined the two horizontal strokes on F with a slightly curved down stroke to get P; rounded off UC into OO, and joined up the top of K so it became R. It now said 'POOR'. Why I thought this would fool my parents is beyond me now. Maybe I hoped they'd believe a fellow secondary modern school write-off had read it and given a damning critique.

My big fear was that Fieldy would embarrass me one Sunday afternoon. He hadn't cottoned on that it was polite to adjust your language to suit the sensibilities of people who might be listening, particularly adults. And he had an unusual vocabulary; a mixture of swearing and inoffensive words in surprising combinations, wherever he happened to be. On hearing the gate click, I'd hurry out and meet him halfway up the path. But one day I didn't hear him coming and there was a loud knock on the door. When I opened it Fieldy shouted: 'Alright, prick dust?' As I put my finger to my lips in a desperate attempt to shush him, I glanced through the crack and Mother and Dad were shaking their heads as they cleared the table after lunch.

That same year when I was ten, Carol, a friendly girl in my class at junior school, invited me to her birthday party. I don't know if she had told her lovely jolly mother that I liked one lass in particular but it looked that way, because in one party game I was thrilled when, smiling knowingly, her mother handed me a forfeit that said I had to choose a girl to kiss. To squeals from all the others, I chose blushing Freda.

Then, after shushing everyone quiet, Carol's mother asked the five or six boys at the party to put up our hands if we knew 'Sixteen Tons', a popular song at the time. All our hands shot up. I liked the singer's name – Tennessee Ernie Ford – and the song made me proud because, just like the song's hero, my dad worked down a mine and, kneeling in a seam a few feet high, shovelled sixteen tons of coal a day. I thought Carol's mother was going to play the record, but she said she wanted the boys to sing the song to entertain the girls and I felt the blood drain from my face. I was contemplating doing a runner when I felt her arm around my shoulder. 'You'll be alright, love,' she said, smiling. 'You'll enjoy it.' And I did enjoy standing with the other boys as we all belted out, 'You load sixteen tons, what do you get, another day older and deeper in debt.' For a few seconds, I even carried the song when the other boys momentarily forgot the next line. In the last verse, after singing 'Saint Peter don't you call me 'cause I can't go,' we all dropped our voices real low for the final, 'I owe my soul to the company store.' Led by Carol's mother, all the girls enthusiastically applauded us.

I had a friend who lived in Tinker Lane called Bob Dickenson. Although he was three years older than me we got on well, he treated me like a younger brother. I used to go to his house and he would show me his dad's spare glass eye, which was kept in a drawer in a sideboard in their front room. We played Subbuteo, both of us kneeling on the carpet flicking plastic players on their weighted bases at the ball and trying to score in each other's goal. Bob, a Sheffield Wednesday fan, once took me on the supporters' bus to watch a match. At one point, two St John's Ambulance men came into the crowd to give first aid to a fan who'd collapsed. Bob laughed when I asked him if the fan fainted because Derek Dooley, Wednesday's centre forward, had missed an open goal.

Although we both attended St Peter's Church, Bob never went to Sunday school, just sang in the choir during services. When I told him I'd enjoyed singing at Carol's birthday party, he said he would take me to choir practice and if I was good enough I would be able to join it myself. A few evenings later, we walked up Law Hill whose gaslit street lamps ended halfway up, so it was really dark as we neared the church. Overhead, clouds raced across a full moon and black bare trees bent in the wind, as we headed across the graveyard towards the shining stained glass windows. The creaking branches had scared me, but standing in a pew next to my friend and singing along I felt safe and happy.

That is until the choirmaster called me out to the front where, before the altar, large stained glass window behind him, he sang a note and asked me to repeat it. I did, but so quietly he told me to sing up. I was so shy and nervous I missed the note. He sang another. Again I repeated it, again out of tune. I could hear the boys chuckling. The choirmaster carried on up the scale, singing a note and asking me to repeat it. The lads in the choir had really

Growing up – Richard with his brother Barry, on a family holiday

got the giggles now, some were laughing out loud. I looked for Bob, searching for support but even he was laughing at me.

I'd always sang along at junior school. For Harvest Festival, autumn produce ... vegetables ... fruit ... a few sheaves of golden wheat ... was displayed in the hall and I particularly enjoyed it when we all sang: 'We plough the fields and scatter, the good seed on the land...' At the end of each school day, after the class teacher told us to put our chairs on our desks, she'd say, 'Hands together, eyes closed,' and then we'd sing: 'Now the day is over; night is drawing nigh; shadows of the evening; steal across the sky." I loved participating in that daily ritual. Once a week, our class would join another class in the assembly hall for a singing lesson.

After my church choir experience, instead of singing as I'd always done I just mouthed the words. Noticing this, our teacher Miss Robbo, as we'd nicknamed her, lifted her hands off the piano keys mid-song and said: 'Richard, I want you to sing.'

Once again I was the focus of attention, but this time because I *wasn't* joining in. In church, a dozen or so grinning youths had added to my humiliation. Now, some sixty ten-year-olds turned their head to stare. Shy by nature, embarrassed, my heart racing, I turned to a lad beside me and whispered: 'She'll have to want.'

'What did you say?' Miss Robbo asked.

'He said you'll have to want Miss,' shouted a lad nearby, who had overheard me.

Girls gasped and covered wide-open mouths as they feigned exaggerated shock; boys grinned at each other. Infuriated by my rudeness, Miss Robbo shouted: 'Get out. I'll deal with you later.'

I was standing by her desk when she came into the classroom. She seemed to smile at me when she sat down. She had always treated me kindly and I thought she was going to ask why I didn't sing and give me chance to apologise. Looking back, I wonder if she felt she needed to assert her authority, that if she let a lad get away with such bad manners it would make it difficult to control her own class, let alone sixty kids in a singing lesson in the school hall. Whatever the reason, she shot to her feet, grabbed me by my arm, pulled up the leg of my short trousers and slapped me hard across the back of my thigh six or seven times.

Miss Robbo's punishment didn't make me sing the next time we were in the school hall. As before, I mouthed the words. Perhaps realising I could never be beaten or coaxed into singing, she didn't check whether I was singing or not.

8.

I HAVE A COPY OF *The Observer's Book of Birds*. It long since lost its dust cover and the spine on its orangey brown hardback is broken. In the top right-hand corner are printed the words 'BOYS' SECONDARY MODERN SCHOOL. KIRK BALK. HOYLAND. BARNSLEY'. Below, a handwritten inscription in blue ink reads 'Richard Hines, Form 1B, Prize, 2nd in exam, July 1957' and in the bottom right-hand corner there is a signature: 'W. Roby, Headmaster.'

All the boys called him Ben. Even before I became a pupil at his school, in September 1956, I'd heard many stories about him from older boys. According to one, an electrician's backside had been sticking out from under the stage as he worked in the school hall. When Ben walked in, thinking it belonged to a pupil he gave it a thrashing with the cane he carried around with him. Another lad, on his way to the sports field to practise putting the shot, accidently dropped the eight-pound lead he was carrying outside Ben's office. Moments later the door flew open and out he marched yelling, 'Cannon to right of them, Cannon to left of them.' It was only when I got interested in poetry that I realised he was quoting from Tennyson's *The Charge of the Light Brigade*.

Today, the school has been demolished and, sixty years after failing my eleven-plus exam and becoming a pupil there, I've driven back over to Hoyland, parked the car, and walked down the road, Kirk Balk, beside which it once stood. Nowadays the site is just a large area of grass, beyond which is the school built to replace it. The old brick boundary wall is still here, the peeling flakes of green paint on railings running along the top looking as if they are from the same paint that coated them when I was a pupil. A few yards further on, some familiar red brick gateposts topped with stone are still there, its gate last locked years ago as I discover on trying to turn its door knob-style handle.

Twenty or thirty yards beyond this gate was the playground in which I joined several lines of boys on my first morning here. And before us, frequently checking his gold pocket watch while he organised us into classes, was my new headmaster, Ben.

I had been expecting a big muscular man who towered above us, but he wasn't much taller than most of us eleven year olds. In fact he was plump, bald and wore round gold-rimmed glasses. Even so, I was scared of him and could feel my heart thumping and blood rising to my face as he called out my name and told me to join the line of boys who had been put in 1B.

I suspected Bob Dickenson had been embarrassed on my behalf when he'd laughed at my singing in St Peter's Church, so we stayed friends. He was now a fourth year and, in the morning break, left his mates standing around in the bike shed and sought me out in the playground to tell me he was a 'server' in school dinners and that I could have a permanent place on his table.

Lunch was eaten in the school hall, with at least a hundred kids wandering around. I was relieved when Bob spotted me and fetched me to his table. It was only when the majority of lads were sitting down that I appreciated he was looking out for me.

The dozen or so lads who hadn't managed to find a place waited at the front until any servers who had spare places raced across the hall and competed with each other to grab a lad and take him back to their table. Finally, there were three boys left in front of the hall in full view of everyone now seated. A lad whose glasses were held together by sticking plaster was grabbed first. That left a lanky kid with amazingly long legs who had been in a newspaper as Britain's tallest schoolboy and a small desperately poor-looking boy, whose black hair looked as if it hadn't been combed for months. To cheers from the tables, two servers then ran across the hall as if their lives depended upon it and the one marginally in front grabbed the Tallest Schoolboy in Britain. The losing server sullenly walked back to his table, leaving the boy with the hair, head hanging in shame, to follow him across the hall.

Then a chant started – 'Grouse ... Grouse ... Grouse ... You've got Grouse' – that I didn't understand until it dawned on me that was the name of the boy nobody wanted to sit near. And that the older ones at other tables were chanting, pointing at and taunting those he joined to eat his lunch. The two teachers on dinner duty shouted 'QUIET', 'QUIET', but the pointing and chanting of the poor lad's name went on until they finally regained control.

I had wanted to go to school in jeans, sneakers and an open-necked shirt, the way I dressed at home. No chance. Mother made me wear a jacket, neatly pressed short trousers, knee length stockings and Clarks shoes, measured to fit my feet. I felt as if I was on my way to Sunday school not a secondary modern where some of the lads wore tattered, handed down clothes and boots with steel studs in the soles. The vast majority were friendly. Even so, there were a few bullies from other villages who didn't know me and, thinking I was a sissy due to my clothes, picked on me.

One was a fellow first-year called Eggy. Bigger than me, each time he saw me in the playground he ran up bellowing at the top of his voice like a crazed bull, then, staring aggressively, his eyes wide open like a Maori warrior, he'd push me hard in the chest. Every time he did this, roaring into my face, although scared I felt a surge of rage against the injustice of his behaviour. The next time he did it, I decided, I'd put up a fight and even if he gave me a beating I'd try and land a few blows, which might stop him picking on me.

I hadn't seen Eggy in the morning break and was queuing to go into school dinners when a hard push in my back knocked me out of the queue and sent me sprawling in the playground. Looking up, I was expecting to see Eggy but it was a blond-haired kid called Wilf. The anger I'd been stoking up all morning in preparation for a fight surged within me. Jumping to my feet, I grabbed Wilf around the neck, held his head under my arm for a few seconds, and threw him on the tarmac. My rage drained away as quickly as it had risen and at first I feared he might jump up and give me a thumping. Instead, he rose slowly to his feet and, without looking at me, walked to the back of the queue. Flattening him seemed to have worked in my favour. Maybe Eggy heard about it, but whatever the reason he stopped bullying me.

No one else did either, until a few months later in the school toilets at break.

I'd just stood up from having a drink from a tap when, looking in the mirror above the sink, I saw a lad called Stennie. He was in the year above, so bigger than me. As I walked past he grabbed me by the lapels of my jacket and pushed me against a wall. Moments later, I felt my feet leave the floor as he pushed me up the shiny white tiles and repeatedly banged my head on them as he shook me. Shocked by this sudden outburst of violence I was momentarily paralysed, until a surge of rage kicked in and I swung my right arm. My fist hit him in the nose and sent a spray of blood on to my shirt. With a look of panic, he let go of my jacket and, as I slid down the wall and got back to my feet, took a hankie from his pocket, held it to his hooter and ran out of the toilets to report me to Ben.

Who, after the bell had rung to signal the end of break, sent for me from my class and gave me four strokes of the cane.

At the time, I thought there was something not quite right about the unrestrained way he had attacked me, then run off to report me to the headmaster. It was as if this big terrifying thug had suddenly morphed into a child. One day, in break, I was standing in the playground with a couple of mates when a tennis ball rolled up to my feet. Moments later, this Stennie ran up to me and, smiling anxiously, asked if he could have his ball back. When I said yes, he nodded a few times as he thanked me, then picked it up and ran back. I caught a glimpse of his vulnerability and my heart softened towards him.

Today, we might suspect he had learning difficulties. Although I couldn't articulate it at the time, even back then as an eleven-year-old I seemed to sense that he had problems. He was in the D form, the lowest in school, and probably struggled to read and write. Big, awkward and used to being bullied himself by older lads, I wondered if full of pent up anger he resented me in my posh clothes and saw beating me up as a way to win status with other kids.

Of course, I will never know why he attacked me. Even now, sixty years later, the memory of his sudden vicious assault is so vivid that had our old school not been demolished, I could walk through the entrance where I am standing, enter the toilet block, and point to the very spot on the white tiles where Stennie had lifted me off my feet and repeatedly banged my head on the wall.

9.

WHEN I WON A SCHOOL PRIZE in my fourth year at Kirk Balk, I once again choose a bird book, this time *The Observer's Book of Birds' Eggs*, which I have in front of me now.

On the flyleaf, handwritten in black ink, it reads: 'Form U4. 1st Place, awarded to Richard Hines.' In the bottom right hand corner it is signed 'W. Roby Headmaster. July 1960.'

After doing well in end-of-term exams in my first year, I had been moved up from the B to A stream. Now in 4A, I was taught history by Ben. This was our headmaster's specialist subject and his informed passion for it made lessons engrossing. Once when Ben praised the work I'd written in my exercise book, the lad next to me, who like all us boys spoke in our local dialect, said: 'He likes thee, Ben.' He did seem to like me and I became his errand boy. If he needed anything doing he would send for me.

One afternoon I was in a lesson when the door flew open and Ben marched in and shouted, 'Hoyland ought to be wiped off the face of the earth.' As his gaze swept the classroom we sat at our desks hoping we wouldn't be the one his wrath descended on. His eyes settled on me. 'Hines. Come with me,' he ordered, then, turning quickly, he marched out of the classroom and left the door open for me to follow. When we arrived at his office he told me to wait outside with a kid called Taylor. A few moments later he came out of his room carrying an envelope and, glaring at Taylor, said, 'This boy has just tried to hang a first year from the goalposts.' Then, handing me the letter, he told me to take Taylor home and give it to his mother and tell her he'd been expelled.

These days it would have been a police officer escorting Taylor, not fourteen-year-old me. As we walked to his house in Longfields Crescent I asked him: 'What did tha do that for?'

'It wasn't me.'

'How come Ben's expelled thi then?'

'I was only holding the rope. It was this other kid that put it around his neck, threw it over the goalposts and lifted him up on to his shoulders.'

'You could have killed him you daft sods ... he'd have been petrified.'

Looking genuinely bewildered, Taylor said: 'I can't see what all the fuss is about ... we were only messing abaht. And if that kid had tipped him off his shoulders – which he wouldn't have – I'd have let go of the rope.'

Taylor's mother knew what all the fuss was about when she opened the envelope and read the letter explaining why Ben had expelled her son. As I walked up the path I could hear her as she shouted at him, and told him he'd shown up the family and asked how he could do such a cruel thing, and demanded to know the lad's name so she could apologise to the poor boy's mother.

Once Ben sent me on a home visit which, today, would have been carried out by a social worker. That morning, a lad entered the classroom and told the teacher the headmaster wanted me in his office. When I arrived, Ben handed me a piece of paper and told me to go to this address and bring back to school a second year boy who hadn't attended for three weeks.

Crossing Kirk Balk, the road beside the school, I walked into a red-brick 1930s council estate and found the house where this twelve-year-old truant lived with his grandma. It was she who answered my knock on the door. 'Good luck to you,' she said, when I told her the headmaster had sent me to take her grandson back. Then, leaving the door open, she went back inside. I could hear the lad arguing with her. Eventually, grinning, he came and stood in the doorway.

'Why doesn't tha come to school?' I asked.

'I don't like it.'

'So what?'

'I'm not going.'

'Tha'll grow up daft.'

'Tell the teachers to send his lessons home for him to do,' his grandma shouted from inside the house. The lad liked that idea and nodded his agreement.

'What if tha gets stuck?' I asked.

'Mi grandma'll show me.'

Reflecting for a moment on what he'd just said, he laughed.

I couldn't persuade him to come back to school, although he did promise he'd make his own way in the afternoon. When he closed the door and went inside I didn't think I'd see him again. But he kept his promise and when I saw him in the playground and smiled at him the returned truant grinned back shyly.

Although Ben seemed to like me and sent me on such tasks, that didn't stop him giving me a thrashing. Only a couple of weeks earlier he'd given me four strokes of the cane after a teacher had sent me to his office for messing about. Even so, when he needed an errand doing he'd talk to me in his office in a friendly way, although I didn't always realise when he was joking. In the 1950s, a thief called Alfie Hinds was infamous for escaping high-security prison – in fact he got out of three. When the newspapers were full of his latest antics, Ben asked: 'Is that criminal a relative of yours, Hines?'

'No sir,' I replied, unable to believe cane-wielding bellowing Ben could be having a bit of fun.

'Only joking boy, only joking,' he said and, laughing, touched me on the shoulder.

On some occasions after I'd done an errand and reported back to his room, he would confide in me. Once he told me how he used to work late in school, until the time he heard breaking glass as someone broke in while he worked in his office. After that, he said he was too nervous to stay there at night.

One morning I learnt of another of his anxieties.

The metal work room was about ten yards from the school gate. Boys who were late were caned by Ben and I was often late in my fourth year. To avoid a thrashing I'd hurry up the path and past the holly bush, hoping I hadn't been spotted. Most times, though, a window would open and Wee Georgie, the metalwork teacher, would stick out his head: 'Headmaster's room, Hines!'

Feigning disappointment at being caught, I'd trudge up the side of the school as if going off to join the queue of latecomers awaiting their fate before, instead, going into school through an entrance that led to the library and hiding there until I heard the kids come out of assembly.

This particular morning I heard footsteps coming down the corridor. Putting down the book I was reading, I stood with my back to the wall near the door, so whoever it was wouldn't see me. As two teachers walked by I was surprised to hear Fred, the English teacher, call our headmaster Ben, like we did, as he told the other teacher Ben had a brother with Down's syndrome and that he dreaded the kids at school finding out.

Having betrayed my own poor Auntie Hannah for fear of her being abused, walking home from Auntie Kath's, I understood his dread of walking through the village and hearing mocking and offensive shouts. Ben's secret stayed safe with me.

I don't recall why, but our art teacher, Idle Jack, hit me at least six times across my backside with a large blackboard T-square once, then bellowed: 'Get back to your seat cretin; you imbecile.' I looked the words up in a dictionary. Cretin: 'a physically and mentally retarded person.' Imbecile: 'a person of abnormally weak intellect.' Soon afterwards, Idle Jack left to start a business making fibreglass car chassis and was interviewed on the regional TV programme *Look North* about the venture. When asked why he'd left teaching he didn't hold back. The lads he'd taught at our school were nothing to Idle Jack. Sitting in the studio, a grin on his face, he told millions of viewers that the pupils at Hoyland Secondary Modern had been cretins and imbeciles.

Next morning as I walked down the corridor Ben was coming towards me. He stopped and asked: 'See the regional news last night, Hines?'

'Yes, sir.'

'Wasn't good, was it Hines? Having a teacher like that in our school?'

'No, sir.'

Then, shaking his head, he walked off.

Watching an ex-teacher mock his pupils on television must have been a humiliating experience for Ben, as the headmaster of a school publicly shamed. But I wondered if he also resented Idle Jack calling his boys mentally and intellectually retarded. I certainly resented the insult. I was also surprised and disgusted how a school teacher had used such a public platform to use words about his ex-pupils that were crude definitions of disabled people such as my Auntie Hannah and the headmaster's brother.

The last time I saw Ben was in the summer of 1962 when, aged seventeen, I had a summer job working for Hoyland council as a gardener in Elsecar Park. One evening on my walk home, I called in a shop opposite Hoyland Town Hall and when I came out I saw him on the pavement.

'Hello, sir.'

'Hines, isn't it?'

'Yes, sir.'

'What are you doing now?'

'Working on the council for the summer, sir, then I'm starting in the sixth form at Ecclesfield Grammar School in September, to study 'A' Levels.'

'You got 'O' levels at Barnsley Tech then?'

'Yes, sir.'

'Did you pass maths?'

'I need to re-sit that one in November, sir.'

'Rubbish,' he said and then, turning abruptly, he marched off down the pavement muttering to himself.

Grinning, I watched him go.

Once, after I'd been sent to his room by the science teacher for messing about, he looked exasperated as he flicked his cane to indicate I should raise my hand. Thumb tucked behind my first finger, skin nice and loose on my palm, I stood with my hand raised, steeling myself for the first blow. It didn't come. Out of the corner my eye I could see he was shaking his head, as if he couldn't make up his mind whether to thrash me or let me off. Then he stopped shaking his head and angrily said, 'You've got intelligence boy. But it's not human intelligence.'

Swish. Swish.

'Other hand.'

Swish. Swish.

Despite this thrashing and the three or four other canings he'd given me for transgressions, I had affection for him. His history lessons had given me a love of the subject and he'd encouraged me to further my education in Barnsley, which changed my life.

I went on to become a teacher and deputy head, set up a film company to make programmes for Channel 4 and BBC2 that gave a voice to working-class people and then became a university lecturer, teaching television and film screenwriting.

As he walked off down the pavement I felt a pang of sympathy for lonely eccentric Ben, who lodged in a house next to a fish and chip shop and, I'd guess, never found love.

10.

ON THE DINING TABLE, spread out before us, are a few black and white photographs taken when Jackie was a girl and lived in a rented terraced house at 17 Calvert Street, Hoyland Common.

My wife was born there on 12 October 1947. It was midday on a Sunday her mother said, and whilst in labour she could hear some miners laughing and talking together, outside in the street, on their way to the pub.

Like Shakespeare's Romeo, as a child Jackie was 'wedded to calamity'. As a baby, she caught pneumonia. A few years later she fell down the cellar steps, dislocated her ankle, and had it yanked into place without anaesthetic, then had to wear a pot on her leg. But worst of all was when she caught measles at infant school. When she had raging fevers her mother would carry her into her bed, where swirling patterns on dark brown varnished wardrobe doors came alive and moved like snakes, and a Rumpelstiltskin-like figure sat at the bottom of the bed, kicking his heels and laughing. After recovering from measles she was so debilitated her friends wheeled her to school in a pushchair and loved racing her around the playground. Until one morning the pushchair fell over and tipped her on to the tarmac.

Once, when Jackie was at her friend Valerie's house, playing with dolls and sitting on a rug in front of the coal fire, there was a loud rumble. And then – WHOOSH! Soot exploded out of the chimney, covering her and Valerie head to toe and sending Jackie running off home with only her eyes showing.

The photo we are now looking at was taken in Hoyland Common Methodist Chapel, where she went to Sunday school. Smiling shyly at the camera, she wears a new pale yellow dress of bubble nylon and matching hair ribbon. Her mother had taken her to C&A in Sheffield to buy new clothes for the Whitsuntide Walk: an annual parade through the village. She says it must have been taken *after* she'd marched behind the Sunday school banner because her mother had also bought her a pair of pale yellow nylon gloves to match the dress, which she isn't wearing in the picture. This is because, setting off for the parade in the morning, she'd run up Calvert Street, fallen down, scraped her hands on the road trying to break her fall and torn out the palms and fingers.

Jackie's terrace birthplace is somewhere else now demolished; modern bungalows stand there these days. She couldn't find any photographs of the front of their house, but there are some of the backyard, which her dad turned into a narrow garden with a lawn surrounded by paving stones. The house itself was lit by gas lamps high on the walls, each with a small translucent white glass shade. Under that was a white lacelike mantle that covered the gas jet. She remembers her dad striking a match, turning a small tap and reaching up to light them, and how a glowing white light cast shadows in the downstairs room and kitchen. Her parents chose not to light the one in her bedroom, so Jackie took a candle in a white enamel candleholder to bed. Even though her mum or dad were always with her, she remembers feeling scared of the spooky shadows it threw on the walls. One day a few years later, when electricity had been installed, she ran down to the Working Men's Club and asked a man going inside to tell her dad to come home because their new television had arrived. Next day she told

Jackie at the seaside with her mum and dad.

a girl at school about this who said: 'That's nowt – we've had one for years.' Otherwise, Jackie loved her cosy bedroom, with its white and blue dotted wallpaper, blue picture rail, skirting board, and yellow door. Her dad, a bricklayer and handyman, had his workshop in the cellar where he made toys for her: a doll's house, a desk and chair. He also made book shelves for her *Rupert the Bear* and *Heidi* books, set to be replaced while in junior school by novels like *Children of the New Forest, Ivanhoe* and *Little Women.*

When World War Two broke out, her dad was all packed-up and ready to join his regiment when a telegram arrived telling him that instead of joining the army he must report to a Sheffield steel factory. Bricklaying was a 'reserved occupation' and his job was to repair the brick furnaces essential for producing the steel needed to build tanks and bombs. Keeping up maximum steel production was so urgent he had to enter the furnaces to replace damaged bricks while they were still hot. Breathing in the hot dust damaged his lungs and throughout his life there were times when he was too ill to work. When freezing or snowy winters made building work impossible, he was laid off and Jackie would go with him to the woods to collect firewood and carry it home in shopping bags. During such times, her parents were so poor Jackie had to wear hand-me-down clothes. One cold day, her mother sent her to junior school in her cousin Paul's overcoat, which he had outgrown. She went to the toilets in the playground and was about to enter a cubicle when a schoolmate walked in and surprised and shocked said to a girl following her: 'There's a boy in our toilets.' Burning with shame, Jackie ran in the cubicle, locked the door, and stayed there a long time, afraid to come out and face a laughing gang.

Some girls in Calvert Street were from large families and wore their older sisters' cast-offs. They didn't seem to notice, or care, that Jackie wore a boy's overcoat. They were all friends and played together on dark nights under the street lamps. In one skipping game her and three or four girls would stand in a row, while a girl at each end of a long skipping rope turned it and recited:

> All in together girls,
> This fine weather girls,
> When I shout your birthday,
> Please run out,
> January, February, March, April...

Jackie was glad she hadn't arrived in January; those born in the early months of the year were first out. And she recalls how as the month of her birthday came nearer ... August ... September ... she had to concentrate. Then when she heard October called out, after checking the skipping rope was near the ground after her last skip, or high above her head, she'd take a deep breath and jump out, ensuring the skipping rope kept turning.

She also remembers Bonfire nights, faces lit by the flames, the whoosh of sky rockets launched from milk bottles and whirring

Catherine wheels pinned to coal shed doors. But her most vivid memory is the night when her mother squealed, laughed and then winced in pain as a jumping cracker, which appeared to have deliberately targeted her, followed her every step and burnt holes in her nylon stockings.

At Christmas, Jackie's uncles and aunties and cousin Paul would join them in Calvert Street. It was a yearly tradition that Jackie's mother, with her arms raised and the index finger on each hand used as a baton, conducted all present as they each took it in turns to sing a line of the carol, 'On the first day of Christmas'. Jackie and Paul liked it best when it worked out that one of the men had to sing: 'On the fifth day of Christmas my true love sent to me, 'FIVE – GOLD – RINGS'. Jackie's dad and uncles couldn't reach the high notes at that point in the song and their efforts to do so usually ended with them dropping their voices really low, which made everyone laugh.

The son of auntie Alice and uncle Herbert, cousin Paul, was a kind-hearted lad three years older than Jackie. His family lived in a rented stone cottage on Primrose Hill in Milton, a hamlet on the Fitzwilliam Estate. Jackie loved to visit them with her parents. In spring, they'd walk through the fields when the white ox-eye daises and purple vetch were in bloom and the marsh marigolds growing in the stream beside the path were yellow as butter. And when the bluebells were out, creating a haze of purple in Spring Wood, they followed a path beneath the oak trees to see their relatives.

Her dad had done his best to make their tiny backyard into a garden, but when Jackie visited her cousin Paul in Primrose Hill it felt like another world. Their garden had a wooden bench that surrounded the trunk of a centuries old tree. The large lawn had flower borders and a gate led into a vegetable garden with fruit trees and bushes. In summer, garden canes set up like the poles of a teepee were covered with pink and purple sweet peas. Jackie liked their smell and gathered a few flowers to put in a vase on the cottage window sill. Paul picked gooseberries, loganberries, raspberries and strawberries for tea.

In a field beyond the fruit trees was a green shed with tubs of flowers either side of its door, wood smoke rising into the sky from a black metal chimney. To Jackie it looked like a scene from a children's book. Sometimes Paul took fruit from the garden to the man who lived there and Jackie went with him. As the man stood in the doorway thanking Paul for his generosity, Jackie would look beyond him into the shed and marvel at how cosy and homely it was; the neatly-made bed; the wooden chair with a cushion; the wood-burning stove for cooking and heating; pans hung on a wall. It was safe, Paul told her, just as long as she didn't touch the poor man or go inside the shed. He lived in isolation because he had TB – tuberculosis – which was still a dangerous infectious lung disease in the 1940s and early '50s.

Not long afterwards, aged nine, Jackie was struck down by a dangerous infectious illness herself. To begin with, she had a sore throat. Instead of singing and joining in skipping games with her friends, she sat quietly on the door step, watching. Soon though, she developed a raging temperature, winced with pain at the slightest touch of her skin, and her legs, arms and joints ached and chest hurt. Her mother hurried across the street, through the back garden of doctors Eric and Marie Allott and knocked on their door.

Before long, Doctor Eric – well over six feet tall – walked into the bedroom carrying his black doctor's bag. Jackie told him she was frightened because of the chest pains. She remembers how he towered above her as she lay in bed. Having been examined, she listened as he told her mother that Jackie had rheumatic fever; a rare inflammatory disease most common in children that can develop after bacterial throat infections. The immune system goes haywire and attacks healthy tissue. He spared her mother the further fact that it could also cause heart failure. Even in the early twentieth century many children died from the disease.

11.

AT THE AGE OF TWENTY, Jackie suffered another bout of rheumatic fever. One Thursday evening she suggested we watch *Top of the Pops* on television rather than sit in her bedroom listening to the radio. So, with one arm around her back and the other under her knees, I lifted her out of bed and carried her downstairs. As we sat on the sofa together she in her blue and white spotted pyjamas began to cry. The noise, the flashing lights, the singing and dancing, the energy of the young people her age, all brought home to her how debilitated she was, how enfeebled.

I carried her back upstairs to bed.

Jackie's nine-year-old self must have had similar feelings, listening to her friends skipping and singing outside in the street.

The junior school gate had a safety barrier in front of it, which was basically two parallel tubular bars. At playtime, girls would race into the playground in a desperate bid to be among the first to reach them. The first four or five would grab the top barrier, swing under it between the top and bottom one, bend their knees over the top one, and hang upside down with their skirts over their heads and navy blue knickers showing. Jackie had very often been one of the first to do just that.

She also went to dancing classes and loved her red tap shoes, which tied with a bow. The well cover in her family backyard was a circular metal lid about a yard across from edge to edge. This was where she practised and loved to hear the amplified sound of the tappity-tap, tappity-tap, of her dance moves. But being confined to bed for months took its toll. After her illness she wasn't well enough to race across the playground to hang upside down with her friends anymore, or attend tap-dancing classes.

When Jackie finally returned to school she was dismayed by the note Doctor Eric wrote for her teacher, explaining she'd had rheumatic fever and should not take part in excessive exercise as that could damage her heart. Going back to school, she could only sit and watch as her friends raced around the hall in PE and between the bases during games of rounders on the school field.

Mr Mann, her form teacher, did his best to make her feel involved by inventing a job – netball reporter. Perched on the playground wall with a notebook, she'd write down the names of the girls in each team, who passed to who, who jumped up and put the ball in the net and the final score. He intended she would read her report out in class, however having spent so long in bed or sitting about in her room, with only the odd friend calling in, she'd lost confidence and put on weight, felt fat, socially awkward, shy. So he agreed to let Elizabeth Gale, her friend, read her netball report to the class instead.

Furthermore, while her classmates had been coached for their eleven-plus exams, Jackie had been off school for most of the year when she took hers. The result wasn't straightforward. She hadn't passed. She hadn't failed. She was a 'borderline case' and would not hear if she'd be joining her friends at grammar school for weeks. In the meantime, she'd have to attend Kirk Balk Girls' Secondary Modern, on the same site as the boys' school but segregated from it and with a different head teacher.

When results of the eleven-plus 'borderline cases' were finally posted out, the one that dropped through the letterbox of 17

Calvert Street brought bad news, so her mother took her to Storey and Cooper's drapery shop on Market Street and bought her a Kirk Balk girls' uniform instead.

Physically, though, Jackie was much better and soon her and her family flitted from their small terraced house in a van driven by a builder friend of her dad. There wasn't enough room for her to sit with her mum and dad up front, so with Tina, her dog, laid at her feet, she sat on top of a coal bucket in the back. Peering through piles of furniture, she could just about see through the cab window and follow the mile-long journey to their new home; a 1930s-built red brick council house opposite her new school.

Together, we're looking at black and white photographs taken in its front garden. In one, Jackie is wearing shorts and a summer top, arms held straight by her side, heels together. It looks as if whoever took it shouted: 'Attention!' Her mother is in it too, stood beside the front door, number 22 above her left shoulder. There are plenty more such photos and I laugh at the amount.

'Anyone would think you'd moved into a palace,' I say.

'It felt as if we had.'

The first thing to strike Jackie was how light the rooms were compared to the ones in Calvert Street. Walking through the long living room for the first time, she opened a door into a kitchen that had a separate pantry – in the old place food was stored on shelves at the top of the cellar steps. And beyond the kitchen, across a small hall that led to the back door, was an indoor toilet. Racing back through the living room she crossed the front hall and looked in the dining room, then bounded upstairs to view the three bedrooms, two large and one small, and finally the bathroom, which also had a toilet. Luxury.

No more would she have to walk out into the dark on cold winter nights, carrying a torch. Or in summer, have to open the toilet door in the backyard and see the whitewashed walls and ceiling alive with dozens of daddy-long-legs.

12.

SEARCHING THE SKY FOR THE arrival of swifts in early May is an annual ritual for us. Now we were moving to Hove, in 2016, Jackie travelled up to witness the event for the very last time.

Growing up in Hoyland Common, I loved to see them squeal and fly up to their nests in Queen Street, Sale Street and Steel Street. Over the wall in Sheffield, at the bottom of our garden, is a stone chapel and in our first spring here in 1982 I was delighted to discover that swifts nested in its eaves. Built in the late 19th century, generations must have been reared there. A few yards beyond it, there is an 18th century cedar farm with a magnificent sycamore tree. Today, only the farmhouse has survived, but in the 1700s the barn and buildings occupied the site of the chapel, so that is where swifts would have nested back then.

Using the sun, stars and Earth's magnetic field to guide them, every August these birds fly thousands of miles to South Africa, then come back the following spring to rear their young in the very same nest holes. In the final stages of their mammoth journey they are said to use local landmarks to guide them home on arced flickering wings; their unmistakeable high-pitched twittering chirps accompanying the swifts' ascent to those familiar eaves.

Flying in from the south over the Peak District, perhaps the first thing they recognise is the heather moor, with its patches of white cotton grass at this time of year. Then the spire of Ecclesall Church, with its Norman arched doors. In the eighteenth century they must have spotted the thatched roof of the farmhouse and, in the nineteenth, the blue slated roof of the stone-built Methodist chapel. In the spring of 1908, the swifts would have seen our row of newly-built terraced houses for the first time.

In *The Homing Instinct*, biologist Bernd Heinrich writes of how for all animals, including humans, home is a 'nest'. It is where we live, where our young are reared, the place we are homesick for, if displaced. Come spring, swifts return to their ancestral homes driven by instinct and emotion. I feel an affinity with that. They connect me to my birthplace, to my dad and brother Barry, who would both look to the skies in anticipation of their arrival, and my ancestors, who would have heard them squealing above the streets. Sometimes they arrive on my birthday, May 3, which is a special treat. When the weather is poor they might not arrive until mid-May. This year, Jackie noted the date in her diary:

> **Thursday 5 May 2016.** *Warm and Sunny. Saw one swift through kitchen window – flying high.*

'They're back!' Jackie called, and we hurried into the garden to get a glimpse of the single swift.

> **Friday 6 May 2016.** *Heard and saw six swifts flying over the garden.*

We'd watched them fly fast and low overhead; some alighting and momentarily clinging to the stone wall beneath the chapel nest-holes. Other swifts soared high up into the sky, flights alternating between bursts of flickering wings and glides; their wings and streamlined bodies pitch black against the expanse of blue.

13.

ON THE TABLE WE HAVE a photograph cut out of an edition of *The South Yorkshire Times*. Jackie, aged fifteen, is wearing her school uniform and smiling shyly as she holds two books. Next to her is a tall blonde girl, being handed a book. The caption beneath says: 'Proud moment for Janet Lomas as she receives the four-year attendance award during the speech day at Hoyland Kirk Balk Girls' School. Looking on is Jacqueline Knowles, with prizes for art and history.'

Also in the photo is a woman wearing glasses and a hat. This is Minnie Gillis, a local Labour councillor. Jackie is five foot three and the top of Minnie's head barely reaches her shoulder. Prize-giving over, Minnie then addressed the hundreds of assembled girls in the school hall and Jackie remembers this tiny woman up on stage and commencing her speech with: "I'm only a little woman, but I am equal to any man." How inspirational.

On the table we have the art prize book Jackie was awarded that day, *Dutch Painting*, which we will also be taking to Hove. Her love of painting and drawing was encouraged by Miss Haigh, her art teacher. When she was in her last year at Kirk Balk, if she didn't like the subject of the next lesson she would tell the teacher

Six-year-old Jackie in chapel, above, in the second row of children from the front, fifth from the left. And, below, after falling and ripping her gloves.

Miss Haigh had said she could finish a painting, on an easel in the corridor. Miss Dunnett, the headmistress, would often stop and admire her work. She even took one of Jackie's paintings, a vase of daffodils, to display on her office wall.

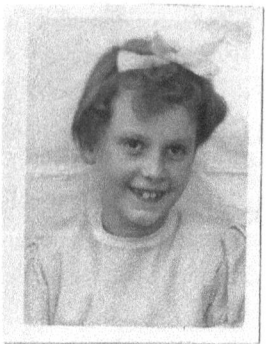

For Jackie, being able to spend so much time doing what she loved in her final summer term at Kirk Balk was great, but she would be leaving in a few weeks. The careers advisor had taken her class on a visit to a 'typing pool' in Newton Chambers, a factory that made toiletries and chemicals. Rows of women spent all day tapping on typewriters. She didn't want to do that, but she had no idea of what job she did want to do.

By chance, Jackie had been talking about this with her mother when Sally Button, a friend from Calvert Street, called in to see her and emphasised to her mother that Jackie was really good and that she should try to do something that utilised this talent. Jackie's mother like her paintings and sketches but her daughter was a secondary modern school lass without qualifications – eleven-plus failures left school at fifteen and didn't take exams. What could she do? Yet in the end it turned out that Sally's chance visit that day gave Mrs Knowles an idea.

Jackie comes from a working class family; her dad was a bricklayer and her mother worked in a fish and chip shop. Even so, they had middle-class relatives on her mother's side. One, her great-aunt Jessie, taught soft furnishings on an art course at Worksop College – we have a photograph of her in a long stylish flowered dress. This connection meant Jackie's mother had heard of art courses – many working-class women wouldn't have – and so she went to ask Miss Haigh and Miss Dunnett if they thought Jackie was good enough to apply. She was delighted when both teachers recommended that she absolutely should.

A couple of weeks later, carrying a portfolio of her work, she boarded the bus to Barnsley before, around twenty minutes later, walking up Market Hill, past the Town Hall, then turning left opposite Cooper Art Gallery. Walking past mature trees, their green leaves still fresh in early July, she reached her destination – a large stone house with two bay windows either side of its front door. The room on the right was the office of Mr Glover. She still recalls the Principal's large ginger moustache and tweed jacket, and how her heart raced as she watched him spread examples of her work on his desk and look at them for what seemed like ages, before turning and welcoming her to Barnsley Art School.

The leaves of the mature trees were beginning to turn golden when, in September 1962, aged fifteen and dressed in a new navy blue duffle coat with wooden toggles, she walked the same route with other duffle-coated students ahead of her first term.

In fact, it was the very same coat she had on some three years later when, on 13 October 1965, the day after her eighteenth birthday, we happened to meet in Barnsley town centre.

'Hello,' she said and then blushed when I asked if we knew one another. She had seen me in Hoyland Common a few times, she said, as we travelled back to the village on the bus.

The following evening we were on the bus again, going to a nearby village, Chapeltown, for a drink in the Coach and Horses, a cosy pub with a blazing fire. When I helped her off with her coat and said I liked her purple dress, she told me that as well as doing art in Barnsley she designed and made clothes and had made this one herself. I was aware of how shy she was, how softly spoken, how hesitant in weighing her words. When she began to relax she told me how, over the summer holidays, she'd worked as a waitress in Bridlington with her art school friends, Pam and Susan, and while there had seen the rock band Eric Burdon and The Animals live on stage singing 'The House of the Rising Sun'.

The girls shared an attic room in a café with three floors. She told me how, dressed in a short-sleeved black cotton dress and white apron with lace edging that she made herself – we still have it in a drawer upstairs – she waitressed on the third. The kitchen was in the basement and Melvin, the chef, sent the food up in a dumbwaiter. There was also a small kitchen in the top café with a telephone and when Jackie's favourite song 'Help', by The Beatles, came on the radio in the basement, Melvin would ring her floor to let Jackie listen to it. She also served desserts and on occasion helped herself to ice cream and a mince pie. One day a tray of pies went missing and Susan told Melvin that Jackie had taken them. He ran up to the attic and lay on his stomach in his black and white checked chef's trousers looking under her bed. It wasn't there of course, Susan had been joking. We were so engrossed telling each other about our lives that when 'time' was called we had to hurry to catch the last bus to Hoyland Common, where we got off at Allott's Corner and I walked her home.

On Saturday, passing borders full of pink and yellow autumn

flowers, chrysanthemums and Michaelmas daises, I walked up her garden path and knocked on the door. Jackie answered and although we'd had a lovely night in the pub, laughing and talking, she still blushed as she asked me in and cleared away a dress she had been making. She let Bobbie, her blue pet budgie, out for a fly around. I really liked her as I watched her gently talking to him as she carried him across the room perched on her finger, then let him hop on to a perch in his cage.

On Sunday afternoon, I called for her again. It seemed there was an unspoken agreement we were now 'courting'. The sun was a ghostly white disc in a high mist, but it was warm as we walked hand in hand past St Peter's Church and into Hoyland Common. She steered me right at Lax's fish and chip shop on the corner of Calvert Street and showed me where she'd lived before. It turned out we had that connection, my great-grandad Hines having lived in the same brick terrace and possibly the same house.

We walked through the fields to Tankersley Church, with its square Norman tower, and sat on a bench beside it. Jackie used to walk to the church with her dog, Tina, and liked the spot as across the fields on the horizon, rising from the trees, was the spire of Wentworth Church next to the school her mother went to when her grandad was a tenant farmer on Wentworth Estate.

After leaving the church, we walked down a stony cart track and stood looking across a field at the ruins of sixteenth century Tankersley Hall. I pointed to a nest hole high in its crumbling sandstone wall and told Jackie that's where Kes, my kestrel, had come from in late June that summer. A lad called John Grayson and me had borrowed a ladder from a building site to climb up late at night because we were trespassing and wanted to avoid being caught by the farmer who lived next to the ruins.

We then turned from the Old Hall, walked across the track and climbed over a stile into Bell Ground Wood. The ground either side of us was covered with autumn leaves. Reaching the edge of the wood, we continued along the path through a stubble field, climbed over another stile and walked to my brother Barry's house, where I kept my kestrel in his garden.

Jackie had read about Barry in the *South Yorkshire Times* after he'd had a play broadcast on radio and knew him by sight. By then he was a PE teacher in Barnsley and she travelled on the same bus as him to art school. Asked about him now, she recalls his striking blue eyes as he stood in the aisle, one hand holding the rail above his head, the other a novel he was reading. When we arrived, Barry and his wife Margaret were reading the Sunday papers outside as I introduced them to my new girlfriend.

The corrugated iron air raid shelter I kept my kestrel in was at the bottom of their garden. I'd fitted a wooden door to it that had a window with vertical wooden slats. When I carried Kes out Jackie marvelled at her beauty; her curved beak, her large brown eyes, her buff-coloured breast feathers with dark streaks, her yellow legs with their black talons gripping my glove.

We walked through a nearby gate and before us a patchwork of golden stubble fields stretched towards Rockingham Colliery's slag heap. I let Kes hop on to a fence post. Jackie stood by a hedge glistening with cobwebs and dew and, with the stubble crunching under my feet, I walked into the middle of the field.

'Come on Kes... come on, girl,' I called, slowly swinging the lure – a piece of cord with a leather pad that had meat attached. Kes launched herself off the post and flew in low. Stepping forward with my right foot, I threw the lure into her path. Instead of trying to grab it, wings pumping, she curved up into the sky. Shortening the lure line by pulling it through my fingers, I swung the lure in circles by my side while looking up at the kestrel above me. She flicked over. I threw the lure up. Head first, wings beating furiously, she pursued it, twisting two or three times in the air as she hurtled downwards. Then, just as it looked as if she was about to crash head first into the stubble field, she levelled out at the last moment, tried to strike the lure with her talons, missed, and curved back up into the sky, flicking over to begin another

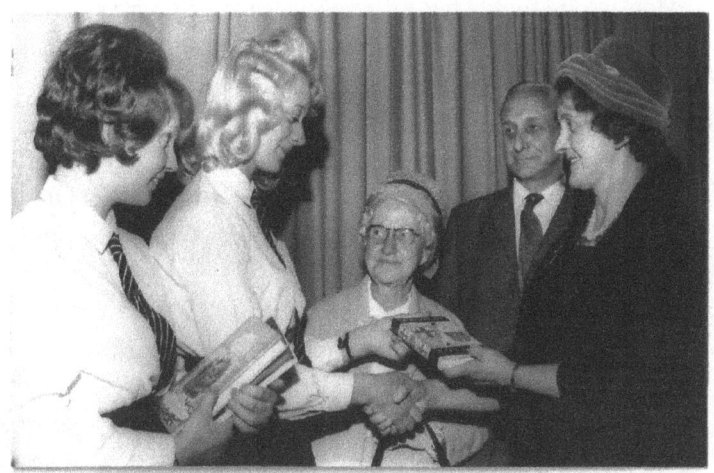

Jackie, on the left, receiving her prize for Art at Kirk Balk Secondary Modern School, aged 15. She then won a place at Barnsley Art School.

vertical stoop. Again, I threw out the lure and kept it tantalisingly out of her clutches as she plummeted head first downwards then broke her descent by curving upwards to begin yet another stoop. And so it went on ... stoop ... after stoop ... after stoop. When at last I eventually let her catch the lure, Jackie smiled as I walked towards her across the field with Kes tearing into her reward of meat on my glove.

There is a photograph from that autumn of 1965 at the start of this book, in which, wearing an open-necked shirt and tight narrow-legged jeans, my hair cut in the style of the Beatles, I have my young kestrel perched on a leather glove Jackie made for me.

Casting my mind back fifty years to that lovely afternoon when I introduced Jackie to my brother, I remember telling her that Barry had told me he was going to write a novel. It was to be called *A Kestrel for a Knave* and be about a secondary modern school lad called Billy Casper, who, just like me, took a kestrel from a ruined old hall to train. I also recall thinking, 'who on earth would want to read such a story?'

How wrong could I be? As is now legend, *A Kestrel for a Knave* went on to be not only an enormous literary success – going on to be translated into languages from German to Japanese – but also become a film that is still beloved the world over.

Along with the photos before me, I also have a copy of the first hardback edition of *A Kestrel for a Knave* from 1968. On the cover a boy is looking up at a hovering kestrel. On an early inside page, the book's dedication reads:

To Richard

And underneath, in ink, Barry has written by hand: 'with best wishes from Barry.'

The first time I saw it, my brother was sitting in the garden reading and I had called around to see him. I asked him the name of the book but he didn't answer. Instead, smiling, he just held up the proof copy of his novel, showed me the title on the front and then opened it and pointed out his dedication. I was touched and really appreciated his kind gesture.

It is, though, surprising Barry ever became a writer.

Six years older than me, when we lived in Tinker Lane as lads, there were no books in our house, except cowboy books by Zane Grey, our dad's favourite author. Barry didn't study literature at school or Loughborough PE College; football and athletics were his thing. Then one rainy day, stuck in his digs, he asked his roommate, Dave Crane, who was studying English Literature, if he had anything he could read. Dave lent him George Orwell's *Animal Farm* and this, Barry said, is what started his passion for reading and gave him the idea to be a writer. When he married Margaret, at first they lived a few hundred yards from us on Hoyland Road where Barry wrote in a spare bedroom, by hand, in school exercise books using a pencil. He didn't have a typewriter. That's how his first novel, *The Blinder*, was written and *A Kestrel for a Knave*, which on film became *Kes*.

Writing *A Kestrel for a Knave*, he'd come out each evening with a notepad and make notes as I weighed, flew and fed my kestrel. We used to go on walks on Saturday mornings and Barry asked me about my falconry experiences, which he later used in his book and screenplay. I told him how I went to Barnsley Library and found MH Woodford's *A Manual of Falconry*, and how I wasn't allowed to take it out because it was a reference copy. Unlike Billy Casper, Barry's fictional hero, I didn't steal it. I went to a bookshop to buy it, ordered a copy, then went back to the library and copied sections out by hand to read while I waited for the book to arrive. There were no photocopiers back then.

One morning, I took Barry on the route I had taken to fetch my kestrel and I told him about that. And how I went with a friend John late at night when the farmer would be asleep, carrying a ladder to climb up to the kestrel's nest in Tankersley Old Hall. In the film David Bradley, who played Billy Casper, got up there by climbing on pegs hammered into the wall. On that moonlit night John and I went to take our kestrels from the nest, John struck up a conversation with a hooting tawny owl in Bell Ground wood. Barry put this in his novel but Ken Loach and producer Tony Garnett didn't include it in the film.

Touched as I was on discovering that Barry had dedicated his novel to me, I was equally grateful and even more delighted in the summer of 1968 when he got me a job on the film as falconer. My task was to train the three kestrels used in the film and teach David (aka Billy) how to fly a kestrel to the glove and lure. Each of the hawks responded on hearing 'Come on, Kes', but I gave them individual names, an idea that came from a story my dad told me. At the pit where he worked three pals, always together, walked into the canteen and someone shouted: 'Here they come: Freeman, Hardy and Willis.' It was the name of a shoe shop and amused me, so Freeman, Hardy and Willis the kestrels became.

Actor David was just 15 during the making of *Kes*, I think. He was a lovely lad, I was full of admiration for him; he worked so

On the set of Kes *– actor David Bradley, Richard the hawk trainer, producer Tony Garnett and Richard's brother, Barry, writer of* A Kestrel for a Knave.

hard. After filming all day he would arrive in a taxi at Barry's house in the evening for his falconry lessons and I would take him into the field to fly the kestrels. Then, when we'd finished, he would go home in a taxi to learn his lines for next day.

David did though find it difficult at first. Flying kestrels, he said, was 'ten times the hardest thing I've ever done.' As for me, I was stressed out. It was my job was to make him into a good falconer and if he wasn't any good the film wouldn't work – his character needed to be an expert. But the lad persevered and in the end got really good at lure swinging.

I remember one funny incident. One day, after we'd watched the rushes in the ABC cinema in Barnsley – ie the film shot that day for the crew to check – I was walking through the town with Barry and Tony Garnett. My brother and me had enjoyed what we'd seen and were laughing at the swearing and local dialect.

Tony, though, had a face like thunder. When Barry asked what was wrong he said: 'We'll end up with an X-rated film that won't be understood five miles outside of Barnsley.'

After my first book, *No Way But Gentlenesse: A Memoir of How Kes, My Kestrel, Changed My Life*, was published in 2016, whenever I did a reading from it at book festivals people often asked if Billy's bullying older brother Jud, played by Freddie Fletcher, actually did kill the kestrel at the end of the film.

This is how it was done.

The day before filming, the film's props department gave me a frozen dead kestrel they had got from a museum taxidermy department. I thawed it out in our shed and put on its legs a pair of leather jesses – straps used to hold the hawk.

Ken Loach's way of getting convincing performances from actors was ruthless. Next day he told Freddie Fletcher and me to stand next to David Bradley in the dinner queue at the catering van. We did that and before long Ken came up to me and said: 'Richard, after you've had lunch take Jud to kill the hawk.' David looked at us but didn't say anything. After finishing our meal, making sure that he saw us, we then walked off.

Later, I was holding the dead kestrel under my jacket when Ken told me to put it in the bottom bin while he distracted David. When the sound and camera were running, Ken told David to run down the garden, feel in the first bin, then the second, where poor David, shocked, pulled out the dead kestrel.

Meanwhile, the kestrel Jud was supposed to have killed in the story was sat on a perch in a spare bedroom at Barry's house, as David eventually saw when we took him there. As I walked downstairs with it on my glove, David, in the hall below, said: 'I knew you hadn't killed it and Ken was trying to make me roar!'

The first signed edition of Barry's novel, which I loved, will find a special place on our bookshelves in Hove.

14.

IN TANKERSLEY CHURCHYARD, SOME OF the green lichen and moss-covered gravestones have remained upright, others are leaning. One is at a gravity defying angle, another flat on its back.

Between the gravestones, clumps of pale yellow primroses are in flower. It's a warm day and Jackie and I have driven over from Sheffield to our old haunts, sitting on the same bench we sat on during the weekend we met. In 1973, ten years after my dad died, my mother married widower Bob here in Tankersley Church.

A marriage ceremony with guests would have embarrassed me, and Jackie didn't like being the focus of attention either. For our own wedding we travelled to Barnsley registry office on the bus. Jackie, Barry, Margaret, our two necessary witnesses and last of all myself had boarded the bus at different stops.

Mother's marriage, though, was a grand affair. I was looking forward to being a spectator at it, watching from the pews. Until she asked me 'to give her away', that is, hand her over to Bob, who would be waiting at the altar. She must have had some affection for me because, when I was little, I occasionally awoke to find her lipstick on my cheek. When I was awake, though, she seemed to find showing me affection embarrassing. Perhaps this is why

Richard mother's marriage to Richard's stepdad Bob in 1973 – ten years after Richard's dad's death.

I had never shown her any and why the idea of walking down the aisle with her arm linked in mine filled me with dread. Yet when she asked, smiling, with a look of anxiety in her eyes, I kept my feelings to myself and told her I would.

It must not have been as dreadful as I'd feared because I don't remember a thing about it, although I do recall spring sunlight pouring through the stained glass windows and throwing patches of colour on the stone-flagged church floor. And how, while standing beside the door waiting to escort her down the aisle and hand her over to her new husband, I struggled not to grin at the sight of the organist, an old woman in fancy-rimmed glasses, feet pumping vigorously as though she couldn't get enough air into the pipes, exaggeratedly waving her arms around as she hit each key. Feeling sorry for being distracted and returning to my pew, I also noticed Mother's left hand shaking and realised what an ordeal for her remarrying had actually been.

After all those years in the family home in 'the lane', Mother

Stepdad Bob's dad, seated first on left, whose own dad was head butler to Earl Fitzwilliam, of stately home Wentworth Wood House

would now be moving a five-minute walk away into Bob's post-war semi-detached red-brick dwelling in Tankersley Lane, a road considered to be the posh part of Hoyland Common. Most of its residents were middle class teachers, managers, business people.

Not long after the wedding I called in to see her.

Bob was out and we had a coffee together. When it was time to go, she walked out of the house with me and I stopped to admire the garden. Its borders were full of late spring flowers; purple irises, orange geum, large red poppies. At the far end beyond a long and neatly-trimmed lawn was a vegetable garden. 'A bit different to our backyard down Tinker Lane this, Mother,' I said, smiling.

Now at the top of the drive, I turned and raised my hand to give her a goodbye wave. Instead of turning and going back into the house, she ran up the drive, put her arms around me and clung on, crying, too heartbroken to speak.

I sensed she felt this was Bob's home; one devoid of memories for her. And that as she had watched me walk away she was overcome by an unbearable emptiness and yearning to return to her past. Back to when Dad was alive. Back to where she had brought up Barry and me. Back to where she could knock on the fireback with the poker if she needed help from our next door neighbour.

Back to where all her lifelong friends lived.

15.

BACK HOME IN SHEFFIELD, I've searched out the marriage certificate – dated 26 May 1973 – that made Bob my stepfather.

Name: Robert William John May.
Age: 57.
Condition: WIDOWER.
Rank or profession: SHIPPING MANAGER.

On the line below are Mother's details.

Name: ANNIE HINES.
Age: 56.
Condition: WIDOW.
Rank or profession: SCHOOL MEALS ASSISTANT.

Clearly, Bob was a middle-class professional when he married my mother, the certificate suggesting an upbringing in sharp contrast to her own working-class experiences.

When he died, I had been touched to discover he had left me his prized possession in his will. Although it speaks of his family history, not mine, it's a beautiful object and we will definitely find a shelf for it in our small Hove flat. I am looking at it now. It is in a square brown leather box edged with a gold pattern. Inside its ivory-coloured satin-lined lid is printed: 'BY APPOINTMENT TO H.M. THE KING. GOLDSMITHS & SILVERSMITHS COMPANY Ltd. 112 REGENT St LONDON'. And in a circular indention in the velvet base is a silver pocket watch with a white face and Roman numerals. It was a tricky thing to do, but using my thumbnail I've managed to prise open the back of the watch, across which is engraved:

R.W. MAY

JULY 1915

FROM HIS GODMOTHER

COUNTESS FITZWILLIAM

Bob's Godmother, then, was married to Earl Fitzwilliam. Their stately home was Wentworth Woodhouse, which is only a couple of miles or so from Hoyland Common, our pit village.

In addition to this main family seat, the Fitzwilliams also had an estate and stately home near Peterborough called Milton Hall, and a third such set-up at Shillelagh, County Wicklow, said to be the biggest house in Ireland, as well as a fifty-roomed house in Grosvenor Square in London's Mayfair.

Had Bob shown this pocket watch to an historian or curator, I imagine they would have assumed he was upper class. His well-groomed appearance ... formal jacket and tie ... highly polished shoes ... clipped manner of speaking with no trace of an accent ... make it feasible that someone might have connected him with the Fitzwilliam family. They'd have been right, but perhaps not in the way they might have imagined.

I was an executor of Bob's will and late in his life took care of his affairs, so his documents ended up with me. I have his birth certificate in front of me as well. In the first section, under the heading, 'When and Where Born', the words 'Seventh June 1915, Friar's House Wentworth' are written in spidery black ink. To the right, under 'Rank or Profession of Father', the registrar has put 'Groom of the Chambers [Domestic]'. Bob's father had been 'in service' then. A servant.

As revealed earlier, when Mother was in service before marrying Dad she had lived in her employers' attic rooms. Bob's father, the Groom of the Chambers, or Under Butler, lived in Friar's House, a fine stone dwelling. Every time I visit Wentworth and walk down the tree-lined lane leading to the church, I glance up at the window of the very bedroom in which he was born. A bit further up, behind a neatly-trimmed beech hedge, is the larger home his family moved into when the Fitzwilliams promoted Bob's dad to Head Butler.

My step-father had fond memories of his childhood. He told me how one Sunday morning when he was five or six years old, so it would have been around 1920, his mother was ill, his dad unavailable for some reason and Countess Fitzwilliam called at their house to take him to church. The pews were packed with servants and estate workers all wondering 'who's that little lad holding the Countess's hand walking down the aisle?' When they entered the Fitzwilliams' private pew at the front, the Earl must have been distracted because he didn't see Bob at first. About five minutes into the service he noticed a child beside his wife. 'Who's that?' he asked. 'May's boy,' the Countess replied.

Later, in 1931, my fourteen-year-old mother would have been preparing and serving afternoon tea for her employers. Bob, who was a couple of years older, would have been riding his bike home from grammar school as fast as he could, hoping he could earn a large tip by caddying for the Fitzwilliam's house guests on the golf course in Wentworth Park. Some evenings, having gone into the Big House with his dad, he'd watch from high on a staircase as a procession of lords and ladies in evening dress walked arm-in-arm into dinner.

Bob's dad, as well as carrying out his estate duties, continued to wait on them throughout each summer, travelling south with them to Grosvenor Square for 'The Season' – ie Wimbledon, The Derby, Royal Ascot, an England cricket Test at Lords, the introduction of aristocratic young women into 'Society' and the subsequent debutante balls.

As a girl, Mother never had a single family holiday. When Bob's dad was away in London for the summer, his mother took him to her sister's in the Berkshire village of Cookham, next to the Thames. He enjoyed walking by the river. His most treasured memory was seeing Stanley Spencer wheeling a cart in which he carried his easel, brushes and paints. After Bob's death, while sorting out his stuff, I came across a book of Spencer's paintings. The artist's love of his birthplace, his beloved village Cookham, its people and its landscapes, spoke to me.

Summer season over, Bob, his mother and dad, all came back to Wentworth. The Earl and Countess needed to be home in time for August 12, aka the 'Glorious Twelfth', when shooting began on their grouse moors in Derbyshire.

Bob told me how fond his father was of Earl Fitzwilliam. They had fought together in the mud and bloody slaughter of the First World War, the Earl an officer, Bob's dad his soldier-servant. And according to him the Fitzwilliams treated his father with respect. Even so, he spent his days and often late nights waiting on toffs, while holding a silver tray. It was a subservient and deferential job, forever at the beck and call of the rich and privileged. Yet in an early-twentieth century era of high unemployment for many working-class people, I imagine Bob's dad would have considered himself fortunate to be a butler. He certainly had a more varied and much easier life than my grandad, who spent his days down a mine shovelling sixteen tons of coal a day.

16.

ON THE NIGHT MY MOTHER DIED, I glanced at my watch. It was 10.30pm, the exact time on the same late August day as dad had died thirty years earlier, in 1963. And once again it had been a beautiful night with a full moon.

On black marble in gold letters, their gravestone reads:

Treasured
Memories of
RICHARD LAWRENCE
HINES
BELOVED HUSBAND OF ANNIE
DIED 29TH AUG 1963
AGED 53 YEARS
ALSO THE ABOVE NAMED
AND MUCH LOVED
ANNIE
DIED 31ST AUG 1993
AGED 76 YEARS
RE-UNITED

What I find most touching about this memorial to our parents is that neither I nor Barry had any input in writing it; it had been composed by Bob. Despite grieving for Mother, who had been his wife for twenty years, he had graciously not included himself and referred to her as our dad's wife. I was particularly moved when he'd shown me a draft of what he had written, then asked if I agreed it would be nice to add at the bottom of the memorial that Mother and Dad had been reunited.

Whenever I visit my parents' grave, I find myself looking at the black marble on the gravestone between the memorials of Mother and Dad. To me, in that space is written the invisible story of the thirty years of Mother's life after Dad died in 1963; her ten years of being alone; her twenty years of life with Bob.

When they married, Mother was assistant cook at Hoyland Common junior school. Bob was shipping manager at a local factory, responsible for transporting the toiletries and medicines they produced around the world. He was middle-class, as was his first wife and family. His son, Stuart, was a solicitor and his grandson attended a private school in Sheffield.

Referring to his formal manner, Mother would occasionally say 'Bob's not like us.' Answering the telephone in a clipped stern voice, he would say his surname, May, and then reel off the phone number before waiting for the caller to identify themselves and say and why they had rung. Mother's friends used to say they didn't like to ring her up because whenever Bob answered he sounded annoyed that they had dared to do so.

When I called in to see Mother, Bob, if not busy in the garden, would sit in on our conversations. Mother and I would grin at each other when he didn't get our working-class humour. Once, we were laughing about how my auntie Kath enjoyed betting on horse racing and how, while reading the messages of condolence on her funeral bouquets, I saw one from the local bookmaker, when he butted in and said: 'I can't see what's funny about that.'

On a 1936 slum clearance map, a family friend of my parents who gave it to me has written the names of the occupants of the houses to be demolished. Beside number five Queen Street are Manny and Hannah Hardy. According to Hoyland Common folklore, when Manny was dying in bed and smelt cooking from the kitchen he called, 'That ham smells nice', to which Hannah replied, 'Its not for thee, its for the coffin bearers.' On another occasion, a concerned neighbour who had known Manny was dangerously ill had asked Hannah, 'How's your husband?' To which she had replied, 'He's dead, thank you.' One day when I'd reminded Mother of those stories, and we'd both laughed, Bob had said: 'I don't find that amusing.'

Yet, despite his formality, as I got to know him better I saw a softer, slightly shy side to Bob's character. If he was anxious, he had a touching habit of shuffling his feet and doing small steps from side to side. And he always stroked and spoke gently to any meowing cat he came across. Not long after marrying Mother he had a tragedy. His son, only in his forties, died of heart failure. Not one to speak of or show his feelings, I'd never heard Bob speak of this until a few years later, when he told me that a day had never gone by when he hadn't thought of Stuart.

I never saw Mother show affection to Bob. Even so, I'm sure she was fond of him. But if he didn't already know, one day he found out he would never replace Dad in her heart.

Maybe it was because she had worked for middle-class families as a girl, but Mother didn't have a working-class accent. She was articulate, good looking, stylishly dressed and, having sold our house in Tinker Lane and continued to work after re-marrying, financially independent. She kept in regular contact with her old friends and neighbours and was at ease in the new social circle she moved in, Bob being a member of Tankersley Church. Stanley Brinkman was the rector and Mother struck up a close friendship with him and his wife, both head teachers in Church of England schools. Years later, at Mother's funeral, the rector spoke fondly of her, then laughed affectionately as he told the mourners how she used to question him about religion and the existence of God.

The Labour Party was founded by Christian socialists; maybe Rector Brinkman and his wife were sympathetic to the cause. Mother's politics were rooted in her experiences of life in a mining village. A lifelong Labour supporter, her first political hero was Labour MP Jenny Lee, who was also the wife of Aneurin 'Nye' Bevan, a Welsh miner's son and the minister who implemented the National Health Service in Clement Attlee's 1945 post-war Government. She also greatly admired the spirited Labour politician Barbara Castle, the government minister who brought in equal pay for women in the 1970s.

In the 1980s, aged 67, Mother went to stay for a couple of weeks at the Greenham Common Women's Peace Camp, near Newbury in Berkshire, with her granddaughter, my niece Sally, Barry's daughter, who lived there as part of the protest against American nuclear weapons being stored at the nearby RAF base. Sally and the others lived in shelters made of bent tree branches called 'benders' but, due to her age, Mother got to stay in a caravan. At family get-togethers, Sally would recall, laughing affectionately, how each morning, immaculately dressed and wearing a touch of red lipstick, Mother would emerge with a handbag over her arm looking as if she intended to 'handbag' any copper in the lines of hundreds who dared to arrest either of them. Aged 17, Sally had been thrown into the back of a van once with at least a dozen policemen where, despite begging them not to hurt her, one had almost screwed off her nipple.

Mother would speak up for her principles whatever company she was in, her beliefs sometimes at odds with the politics of the people she met. One friend of Bob's was a Freemason and this man and his wife sometimes invited them to Masonic do's. On one such occasion they were talking in a group when one woman laughed and said, 'You've landed on your feet. A widowed miner's wife marrying Bob and moving up in the world.' Angered by this insult to Dad and their working-class background, she told the now ashen-faced woman that if she thought she was ashamed of her miner husband she couldn't be more wrong. As poor old Bob stood listening, she forcefully went on, saying that nobody could replace her first husband and she would give anything to go back to the days when he was alive and they lived in Tinker Lane.

Not long after I heard about this incident, Dad's Auntie Lena died. I asked Mother the date and time of the funeral. She asked me not to attend. Surprised, I asked, 'Why not?' 'Richard,' she said emphatically, 'I don't want you to go.' Not many people have watched a burial through binoculars, I suspect, but the cemetery could be seen from an upstairs window in our house in Hoyland Common and, sensing I might get a clue as to why she hadn't wished me to attend, it was from there I took my vantage point.

Despite the distance, I managed to follow proceedings clearly: the vicar said a prayer; the mourners threw handfuls of soil into the grave; then Mother walked away to stand by herself. Turning the focus ring, I zoomed in on her. Tears streamed down her face. She was crying uncontrollably.

It seems she hadn't wanted me to see her grief and, although I can't be sure, I think I understood. She had Barry and me to connect her to Dad, but Auntie Lena was the last link to her and Dad's past. He would have introduced Mother to Auntie Lena when he returned from Bradford to lodge with her in Sale Street; as a smiling nineteen-year-old, she would have proudly shown Lena the engagement ring Dad had bought her. In times of mining accidents and tragedies ... the suspected broken back of my dad ... the death of her father ... Lena would have called in to console her. Over the years, shopping in the village, they would have shared Hines family news. In short they had a shared history, but now Auntie Lena had gone.

17.

ON A BRIGHT COLD SUNNY DAY in the winter of 2009, I was standing in front of the Bodleian Library. Nearby a choir sang Christmas carols. I missed my dad, who had been dead for nearly fifty years. Had he seen me standing before this fifteenth century honey-stone-coloured arch, with its two heavy oak doors, he'd have said, 'Who'd have thought it? Our Richard doing a reading at Oxford University?' I'd never imagined I would find myself standing here on my way to read something I had written for *Archipelago*, an occasional Oxford literary magazine which publishes work on landscape and the natural world.

Crossing a paved quadrangle I went through another entrance and into the divinity school. Gazing up at its high fan-vaulted ceiling, I thought, had I been clever enough to become a student here, I would have been overawed by the surroundings and felt out of place. Simon, a work colleague and Oxbridge graduate whose dad is a surgeon, told me there had been a lot of snobbery and working-class students had a wretched time. Now aged sixty two, and with a lifetime of experience behind me, I didn't feel overawed, but I worried my autobiographical piece about life in a Yorkshire pit village might not go down well here.

Andrew McNeillie, the editor of *Archipelago*, had said he would meet me here, along with other contributors who would be reading this evening. I was too early so, to pass time and prepare, I went upstairs and sat at a library table. Looking around at the dark oak bookshelves and paintings of Henry VIII and other kings on the walls, I remembered emailing Andrew to ask him how long my reading should be and having to smile at his reply. It didn't say 'about', 'around' or 'approximately', this being Oxford it had to be in Latin: '...circa eight thousand words'.

I re-read them so many times on the train down that I almost knew it off by heart and after concentrating on a couple of pages my mind wandered to the events that had led me here.

As I wrote earlier, my brother hadn't kept or trained a kestrel himself, but given that *A Kestrel for a Knave* was now on English Literature school curriculums and a Penguin Modern Classic, its iconic reputation further enhanced by Ken Loach's beloved film adaptation, the birds were now synonymous with Barry. At first when I spoke in public on the subject, I'd talk about training my own original Kes and in fact all the kestrels in the film, until that began to feel like an attempt to muscle in on his success. It wasn't his fault of course, but it felt as if he had taken over my identity and so I spoke less and less of my love of hawks. Before long, I made no mention of when I'd been a hawk-obsessed secondary modern school write-off, whose experiences had helped to inspire Barry's book and the film.

In May 2003, biographer Anthony Hayward interviewed me for his book *Which Side Are You On? Ken Loach and His Films*, (Bloomsbury, 2004). The chapter about filming *Kes* is called 'A Wet Weekend in Barnsley'. Barry had told Hayward the idea to give Billy Casper a hawk came from me. I don't remember his first question, but I do know that once Anthony set his tape recorder running he didn't need to prompt me, as I spoke of my boyhood fascination with hawks, how I had trained my own kestrels and my experiences of being the falconer on the film. It felt as if I'd been bottling up my story for over thirty years and that it had suddenly come pouring out. It was that interview which prompted me to reclaim my own tale and today here I was, about to share it again with an audience in the Bodleian Library.

The convention at such Oxford gatherings, I now know, is not to give the reader a friendly welcoming round of applause after their introduction – or clap appreciatively when they finish. Also on the bill was eminent Scottish poet, editor and critic Douglas Dunn, whose beautiful poem *Instructions to a Saintly Poet* goes:

> What do you wish for?
> If it is power put your pen down.
> If it is wealth,
> Do not begin.
> If it is acclaim,
> Lay down your pen.
> Listen to the sunrise
> With your eyes closed.

Like all the excellent writers who read out their work before me, Douglas's words were received in complete silence.

I found the atmosphere intimidating. I had never heard a recording of my own voice and when my own turn came and I stood at the microphone with around eighty people seated in rows before me, it struck me how strong my Barnsley accent sounded as it boomed out of the speakers perched high above its dark and ornate panelled lower walls. Known as Convocation House, the room had housed the Parliament of Charles I from 1642 to1646, when the king was resident in Oxford during the Civil War. I did wonder, rather romantically, whether mine was the first working-class voice to echo around it since Cromwell's labouring-class soldiers routed the Royalists from Oxford. And now here I was, telling them about how I first came in contact with the upper-classes by reading about them in falconry books.

A close-up publicity shot for Kes, *featuring David Bradley and his kestrel*

'Their poshness amused me – "When hawking in India one needs a horse" – and I enjoyed their eccentric antics, such as the aristocratic falconer who flew his goshawk along a corridor past Ming vases and priceless paintings. Yet to me,' I read, 'all that stuff about social divisions belonged in the past. It was the 1960s, The Beatles songs and northern voices were on the airwaves, and accents and class didn't matter anymore. But when I met my first real life falconer I was astonished. It wasn't just his accent that intimidated me, but his confidence, his sense of effortless superiority instilled by a public school education, and his lack of inhibition and booming voice as if he assumed what he was saying would be of interest to everyone within fifty yards.'

At this point something caught my eye on the edge of my vision. Glancing across I saw Andrew, the editor of *Archipelago*, doing a celebratory fist pump and mouthing, 'You tell 'em.'

Trying not smile, I went on:

'Not long afterwards, a lad who'd kept a kestrel told me the experience of a Yorkshire miner he knew. This miner let it be known to a group of middle-class falconers that he was interested in joining their ranks, only to be mocked and snubbed by them. Later, I read of an upper-class army officer falconer who, in the late 1880s, abandoned flying his peregrine on Salisbury Plain to join his regiment and break a strike of half-starved miners like my great-grandad. It took meeting an upper-class falconer myself for me to realise how obsessed I'd been with a history and world in which I would never belong and so I abandoned falconry.'

After I had finished my reading, there was bit of commotion in the audience. A man had risen to his feet and was excusing himself as he hurriedly brushed his way past the rows of seats. I thought he might be hurrying to catch a train, but when he got to the centre aisle he headed straight down it, eyes fixed on me. He was a big well-built man; well dressed, with grey hair. Given the speed of his approach I thought I must have offended him, and he was going to give me a telling off. Then, when he raised his arms, I thought he was going to hit me but, instead, he threw them around me and gave me a hug as if greeting a long lost friend or relative. He then put his hands on my shoulders, pushed me back so he could see my face, and grinned: 'You've met the upper classes, haven't you? And they are not very nice are they?'

It was true and I *had* abandoned falconry after meeting the upper-class falconer, but I still loved hawks and for the next three decades my eyes had scanned the skies in the hope of seeing one.

Eventually, one sighting resulted in an unexpected outcome. Having driven to collect Jackie from work, I got out in the school car park and flying towards me, several feet above the tarmac, wild eyes firmly fixed on my face, was a sparrowhawk. I stood in awe as it flew a couple of inches over my head and away. Its sudden closeness, the sound of its beating wings and rush of air upon my face were too powerful to resist.

And so, thirty years after my last go, I'd decided to fly another falcon, a male merlin, on the moors near my home in Sheffield.

18.

A COUPLE OF DAYS LATER, back in South Yorkshire, what I remembered most vividly of the evening in The Bodleian wasn't my eventual reading, it was the nervous wait I'd endured among Convocation House's polished oak benches.

My piece's title had been *Redeeming Kes, Manning Fanshawe*, so named because the merlin I'd now adopted was named after Sir Richard Fanshawe, the last tenant of the ruined seventeenth century hall among whose walls Kes, my kestrel, had hatched.

It fascinated me that as Secretary of War to the king's son, The Prince of Wales, Fanshawe himself must have sat in the very same room I had; maybe on the exact spot. I'm looking at a postcard I bought there and in front of Convocation House's large arched leaded window is the king's wooden throne, under a canopy. He'd have been among the Members of Parliament surrounding it.

Originally, I'd intended calling my merlin Lilburne, after John Lilburne, leader of the Levellers, who helped defeat the Royalists in the English Civil War – I'd have been a Parliamentarian! But I decided to save that name for a future hawk. Sir Richard was an aristocrat and almost certainly would have set his dogs on me had he caught me on his land taking a kestrel from a nest, but I like to think he might have been understanding of my passion for falconry. My fascination with him began on that moonlit night in 1965 when my friend and I placed the ladder against the wall of the ruins to take our kestrels from a nest in the wall of Tankersley Hall, where he had lived in 1654. An aristocrat in the age of Shakespeare, he would definitely have been knowledgeable about the subject. I'd read a vivid description of how to hood a hawk taken from Edmund Bert's 1619 book, *An Approved Treatise on Hawkes and Hawking*. I loved the idea that over three hundred years ago Fanshawe may have read those very same words and sensed a connection with him over the centuries.

Fluent in several European languages, Sir Richard Fanshawe was a poet who when he wasn't writing spent hours reading. According to his wife, he even 'had some book in his hand' while out walking. He was also brave. Once, strolling with his wife on Portsmouth seafront, they were fired upon by two Dutch ships. Hearing musket balls whizz by, Lady Fanshawe began to run, but Sir Richard went on calmly. 'If we must be killed, it were as good to be killed walking as running', he said.

I have a photograph of a portrait of him that was, I like to think, painted when he lived in Tankersley Hall. Strolling around my old haunts, I sometimes swept my binoculars along the sandy stones hollowed out over four centuries by the wind and on to a herringbone-patterned brick fireplace in the ruins. Then I would imagine him, long curly brown hair, moustache and small goatee beard, seated beside it in a large white lace collar shirt and cuffs, with his black and white greyhound looking up at him adoringly.

This photo is on the front of his wife Anne's book, *Memoirs of Lady Fanshawe*, written in 1676, which I bought in the 1980s from a publisher of rare and out-of-print books. I was captivated. She tells how her husband was captured after the battle of Worcester and imprisoned in a cold, small room in Whitehall, where scurvy 'brought him almost to death's door'. She goes on to say 'every morning when the clock struck four, with a dark lantern in my hand and all alone, I would stand under his window and softly call to him and he never failed to put his head out on the first call.' They would talk together and she tells how: '...sometimes I was so wet with rain, that it went in at my neck and out at my heels.'

One morning, Sir Richard was so ill he asked her to get a certificate from his physician and ask Oliver Cromwell if he could be released on four thousand pounds bail. When she went to the Council Chamber to put her husband's case, 'many spake against it', particularly Sir Henry Vane, who said if he had the opportunity he would hang Fanshawe, who had been close to Charles I. Lady Fanshawe tells how her husband spent time with the king when he was held in Hampton Court Palace before his execution. On a visit to see them both she was so moved by the imminent royal beheading, she cried and the king gently touched her cheek saying, 'Don't cry, dear.' Even so, General Cromwell ordered that Fanshawe be given his liberty for the sum offered. Very ill after his release, when he recovered, Fanshawe visited his friend the Earl of Strafford in Yorkshire, who was the son of Sir Thomas Wentworth, the previous Earl of Strafford, a Royalist executed on Tower Hill in London twelve years earlier in 1641. He offered Sir Richard a house in Tankersley Park, for which he paid a hundred and twenty guineas.

About their move Lady Fanshawe wrote, 'In March 1653, with our three children Ann, Richard and Betty, we went into Yorkshire where we lived a harmless country life minding only the country affairs and the country sports'. One of those would have been falconry. On that night when I fetched my kestrel from the ruins, I'd only learned Sir Richard Fanshawe had lived there from a Tankersley Church pamphlet and anyway flying a hawk was only half of it. I was equally interested in falconry history; the ancient terms, vivid quotes from centuries-old books and Shakespeare. My friend John, who came with me to find a kestrel, wasn't interested in any of this, I don't think he even trained his kestrel to the lure. It felt as if Sir Richard Fanshawe was the only person who would have empathised with my obsession.

More recently, driving over from Sheffield to walk through the woods and fields around Hoyland Common, I ended up sitting on the wooden bench opposite what's left of Tankersley Old Hall. Lady Fanshawe wrote, 'I found all the neighbourhood very civil and kind on all occasions; the place plentiful and healthful and very pleasant, but there was no fruit: we planted some, and my Lord Strafford says now, that what we planted is the best in the North.' Fruit trees still grow in the garden of what is now called Old Hall Farm. Did some of those spring from the seeds of those trees planted by the Fanshawes, perhaps?

Beyond these trees is a stone arch, now blocked off, that was once the gateway to the hall's courtyard. Gazing at this really sparks my imagination. Throughout the spring of 1653, Sir Richard's falcons would have been in the mews moulting. By harvest time, in their new plumage, they would be ready to be flown to catch game; grouse and partridge. And Sir Richard would almost certainly have gone partridge hawking on Hoyland Common, which was part of the Earl of Strafford's estate.

These falcons might have been transported, hooded, on a 'cadge'; a padded square frame on which they would perch. If this method had been used, a 'cadger' (i.e. boy or servant) would have stood in the middle of the frame, put a leather strap over each shoulder, lifted it and carried them. But Hoyland Common was just a few minutes' ride away and I like to picture Sir Richard in the courtyard climbing the stone steps of a mounting block to get on his horse. In the event of which, a peregrine wearing a leather hood with a tassel on top would have been passed up to him before he rode out to hunt partridges for the table.

On the common the swishing scythes would have done their job. In the fields the 'stooks' of the cut wheat and barley would be stood upright to dry. If more than one bird had been carried there, only one peregrine would be flown at a time. When the

Richard's Kes came from a nest in the ruins of Tankersley Old Hall in 1965, the 17th-century home of Sir Richard and Lady Anne Fanshawe.
The couple lived in the hall until their daughter – Ann, but no 'e' – died in 1654.

dogs flushed a covey of grey partridge, the soaring peregrine, wings pumping, would have stooped in a head first dive, then curved into a level flight a few feet above the ground; sometimes its outstretched claws would have grasped its chosen victim, both tumbling to the ground in a frenzy of flapping wings. Often the peregrine would have had to chase the fast flying partridges across the golden stubble fields as they desperately sought cover.

That autumn and winter of 1653, and the following spring and early summer of 1654, when the fruit trees they had planted were covered with pink and white blossom, the Fanshawes continued to mind 'only the country sports and country affairs,' but such a harmless existence couldn't last. In her memoir, Lady Anne tells why she and her husband abandoned Tankersley Hall.

'The house of Tankersley and Park are both very pleasant and good and we lived there with great content; but God ordered it should not last, for upon the 20th of July 1654, at three o'clock in the afternoon, died our most dearly beloved daughter Ann, whose beauty and wit exceeded all that I ever saw at her age. She remained between nine and ten years old and the dear companion of my travels and sorrows, she lay sick but five days of the smallpox, in which time she expressed so many wise and devout sayings is a miracle of her years. We both wished to have gone into the same grave with her. She lays buried in Tankersley Church, and her death made us both desirous to quit that fatal place for us, so the week after her death we did.'

Politically, I couldn't be more against the aims of Sir Richard Fanshawe's side – fighting for a king who believed he had a divine right to rule. Yet as a father and now grandfather, I find Lady Anne's beautifully written and heartfelt description of the loss of and grief over their lovely daughter very moving. I feel as if I knew the child; she could have been one of our daughter's friends when they were between 'nine and ten years old'. One day, as I walked down the cart track past the ruins of Tankersley Hall, I stopped and gazed at the herringbone fireplace and thought of them, Lady Fanshawe, Sir Richard and Ann, warming themselves around it. Remembering how they had 'wished to go into the same grave with her' I understood their sense of loss and how beyond issues like politics and class, what really matters is common humanity.

Since the 1980s, I've been trying to find Ann's grave but my efforts haven't been very successful. One day, I saw the church was open and went in. Reverend Hale was there, but he didn't know about Ann and her history and I couldn't look for a memorial because the stone floor is now carpeted. Since then, in my research of Tankersley Church history, I have discovered the grave is at the foot of the pulpit. Rector Nicholas Greaves, at the church from 1634 to 1678, would have said a prayer as the coffin was lowered into the grave and her heartbroken parents looked on. However, neither I nor anyone else can view it these days because the area in front of the pulpit and altar are also carpeted.

I am a member of a group called Networks for Nature, where scientists, artists and writers interested in the natural world give reports and readings of their work. In 2010, nature writer Mark Cocker invited me to read my *Archipelago* piece in Stamford, Lincolnshire. There were about sixty or seventy people there. From the appreciative receptions given to earlier readings and talks I knew they were a friendly crowd but even so was surprised when I finished and all of them shot to their feet to give me a standing ovation.

Afterwards Mark introduced me to one John Fanshawe, who handed me a book and said, 'I would like you to have this'. On the flyleaf he had written: 'Richard. All thanks for a wonderful talk at Stamford. V.best. John Fanshawe.'

I have the book in front of me. On its blue cover is printed:

THE PEREGRINE
J.A. BAKER
Edited by John Fanshawe

I had read Baker's *The Peregrine* when it was first published in 1967. It alerted me to how organo-chlorine pesticides, such as DDT, passed through the food chain and accumulated in peregrines and other hawks, causing death and reproduction problems. It inspired me to study Environmental Studies at Leicester Teachers' Training College and write my final year dissertation on how peregrines, along with other birds of prey, were facing extinction. In Baker's words, they died 'withered and burnt by the filthy insidious pollen of farm chemicals.'

It was now John's turn do his reading and I didn't have time to ask him what I was desperate to know, namely, was Sir Richard Fanshawe his ancestor? I'd felt connected to Sir Richard through falconry and imagined him as a man who had flown and loved peregrines. What an amazing coincidence it would be if it turned out that John was a descendent of his who cared enough about their plight to edit a book about them. That evening I found out.

A small group of us went to a pub and John sat next to me. He bore no resemblance to the image of Richard Fanshawe on the cover of Lady Fanshawe's memoir, however he did indeed confirm Sir Richard as an ancestor and said how interested he was to know that my kestrel, Kes, had come from the ruins of his 'ancestral home'. John said he hadn't known the family had lived in Tankersley and was really interested in how they came to be there, until Ann's tragic death.

A year or so later, Jackie and I were back in Tankersley, sat on the bench in the churchyard, as we usually do for a while before going for a walk. However on this occasion the wrought iron gate on the church porch was open. We walked over the stone flagged path, opened the arched oak door and entered, instantly hit by shafts of coloured sunlight that shone through the stained glass windows and lit a gloomy interior. A woman was busily doing something around the altar, polishing the silver or dusting. We knew her from previous visits and she left what she was doing to talk to us. She glanced at the carpet in front of the pulpit and said it was spoiling the stone floor and was going to be taken up soon. Jackie, too, is now familiar with Ann's story and my hope of one day having her memorial plaque visible for all to see. I looked at her a moment, before telling the woman about Ann Fanshawe. I then asked if it would it be possible for us to see it, given the carpet was about to go anyway. 'Of course,' she said and knelt to roll it back. And there it was:

Nearby lieth the
body of ANN who
died at Tankersley
Park 22nd JULY 1654
aged eight. She was
the daughter of
Sir Richard Fanshawe secY

Richard's great grandparents John and Sophia.
John would almost certainly have taken part in the 1893 pit yard riot.

Richard, aged three or four, with his mother and dad at the seaside.

*Richard sitting in a meadow of buttercups with his mother
and two-year-old son John, between them, in 1978.*

Richard's mother Annie, aged 70, third from left at a Greenham Common womens' peace camp in a protest against the siting of nuclear weapons there in the 1980s.

Richard with his son, John, daughter Katie and dog, Flick, on a wall in front of the ruined Old Hall in 1984.

Jackie's farming family, the Richardsons, were tenant farmers on the Fitzwilliam Estate.

Left: Elsie, Jackie's mother's sister, with the Richardson's Shire horse that ploughed their land.

Right: Jackie's grandad takes a break with his trusty sheepdog, Fly, as does her grandma Richardson, below

Above: Jackie's mother Dorothy, seated left, with her sister, Mary, on the stone wall in front of the farmhouse as children.

Grandad Richardson working on the farm, left, and, Grandma Richardson feeding the hens, right. Soon after the latter photograph was taken, despite having been a farmer's wife for many years, she was evicted from the farmhouse by the Fitzwilliam Estate.

Jackie standing on the edge of one of the fields her grandad ploughed with his Shire horse, left. In the background we see Wentworth Church spire.

Jackie in 1968, wearing a silk-patterned top, black silk sash and black trousers, an outfit that she designed and made herself.

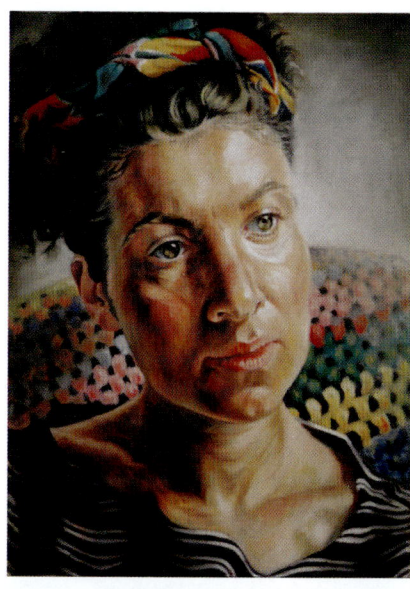

Jackie's portrait of Sonia Garcia Lorus, left, won at the South Yorkshire Open

Richard's merlin falcon Fanshawe, left, who was named after Sir Richard.

Richard Hines with David Bradley, who played Billy Casper in Ken Loach's film Kes. *Richard was falconer for the film and taught David how to fly falcons.*

of war to the Prince of Wales
afterwards King Charles ll

I was sad to see that Lady Fanshawe's name, the mother who had given birth to their beloved Nan – her parents' affectionate name for their lost child – had been left off the memorial.

What also surprised and troubled me was that, according to the memorial, Ann was eight when she died. Lady Anne had written, so movingly, that, 'She was between nine and ten years old, very tall, and the dear companion of my travels and sorrows.' Standing in church and seeing 'aged eight' etched on the brass, I didn't believe it, convinced her mother's account must be true.

But if my gut feeling is right, how could the wrong age of her death have ended up on her memorial? After Ann's death, her mother wrote how they 'quit that fatal place' within a week. In those grief-filled hectic days of sorting out their affairs and arranging the funeral, could Sir Richard have mistakenly written 'eight' on what he wished to be etched by the engraver? Or maybe the latter had made a mistake and the memorial hadn't been laid upon the recently dug grave before the Fanshawe's left Tankersley and were denied the chance to read the finished brass memorial and notice the mistake? Of course, the only person who could explain why Ann's age on her memorial is not the same as that in her mother's quill-written memoir is Lady Fanshawe, whose husband Richard had died before she wrote it in 1679, twenty-two years after the death of her 'most dearly beloved daughter'.

I didn't know John Fanshawe's email address, but have a friend who worked with him at Birdlife International. He forwarded my message, along with the photograph of Ann's brass memorial. In his reply, John thanked me and said it was a delight to have the picture of the plaque and how traumatic the death of Ann must have been for her parents. He could imagine how her loss drove them to leave the house and added how it was lovely to think those walls where they had lived had yielded my Kes.

A nice surprise was the photograph of an oil painting of Lady Anne Fanshawe that John attached to his email. I have it in front me. It shows her as a beautiful woman in her late twenties or early thirties perhaps, wearing a black dress with a low neckline and a wide white lace collar. Her eyes are brown and her black shoulder length hair hangs in soft ringlets. It is painted in the style of portraits of aristocratic ladies in the reign of Charles I by skilled artist Cornelis Janssens van Ceulen, also known as Cornelius Johnson. Yet, to me, this English artist, who moved to the Netherlands to escape the Civil War, hasn't quite captured her character or given any hint of her intellect and tender heart beating in the pale-skinned bosom revealed by a low neckline.

Lady Anne Fanshawe by Cornelius Johnson

That said, now I have an idea of what Lady Anne looked like, on my walks past the ruins of the Old Hall I will be able to bring her to life in my imagination at a time when the Fanshawes 'lived there with great content'.

I can picture a scene in the garden in spring, in which she is laughing and playing with their children under those blossoming fruit trees, Ann, Richard, Betty and newborn baby Margaret, while her husband sits in the shade with 'some book in hand'.

The Memoirs of Lady Fanshawe, with John's email photograph of her portrait tucked inside, John's signed copy of JA Baker's *The Peregrine* and my copy of *Archipelago* will all find a welcome place on the bookcase in our Hove flat.

19.

MY BROTHER BARRY'S MEMORY HAD begun to fail him by the time he reached 70, and he often rang to ask me to help him remember events and people from our past. When I was a teenager and he was in his twenties, we were out walking together when we saw a Jack Russell Terrier chase a hare across a field and heard its owner shout: 'Come here! Tha'll never catch that.' Fifty years later he remembered the dog chasing the hare and what the man had shouted – which had amused us. But on the phone he told me for the life of him he couldn't remember the man's name. When I told him it was Cocker Hardy I could sense his relief.

Over the months and years it became apparent that Barry's forgetfulness was more serious than what most of us experience as we get older; he was diagnosed with Alzheimer's. Once when I took him on a walk he was troubled by an imaginary financial problem and kept repeating he'd talk to Mother about it. Then, holding out his hands, he mimed pushing a document under a screen, saying he needed to go to the bank. When I first visited him at his care home he was in a corridor examining imaginary objects on a blank wall. When he saw me, he walked forwards smiling and said: 'Richard, I'm so glad you've come.' Eventually, though, he no longer recognised me and would chat about his brother 'Our Richard'. His carers said he would occasionally call out my name.

Whenever Jackie and I are on the moors near our home in Sheffield, we always pause and look at the domed top of Hoober Stand, a Grade II-listed thirty-metre-high (98ft) tower on a ridge, four miles distant from where we were born. The monument was built by the 1st Marquis of Rockingham on his Wentworth Estate in 1746, to celebrate the defeat of the Catholic Jacobite uprising at the Battle of Culloden by the Duke of Cumberland's army, in which he served as a colonel. It is believed to represent England, Wales, Scotland and Ireland, all united under one crown, as represented by the dome. Driving out of Wentworth village and through the hamlet of Hoober, it rises out of the trees beside the road. On one such trip to visit Barry, by then resident in a care home in the village of Swinton, his daughter Sally had rung to say her dad was critically ill. When we entered his room he had his eyes closed and was breathing heavily, his chest rhythmically rising and falling. Sally sat beside his bed, reading, I was touched to see, from *No Way But Gentlenesse*, my memoir of how Kes, my kestrel, changed my life.

While Jackie held Barry's hand I told Sally my dilemma and asked her advice. My book had only been published a few weeks earlier in March 2016 and the publishers, Bloomsbury, had arranged newspaper, radio interviews and literary festivals for me to promote it. I'd done a few already. One had been with Jarvis Cocker, founder and frontman of Sheffield band Pulp among much else, who had kindly invited me to be on his *Sunday Service* programme, then on BBC Radio 6 Music. My problem was I had now been booked in for the BBC Radio 4 series *Midweek* too, in the morning at nine o'clock, hosted by Libby Purves. I asked Sally what she thought. Should I cancel it in case Barry died while I was away, or travel down to London later? Looking at her dad affectionately, then smiling at me, Sally said: 'He's overshadowed you in life, now he's threatening to overshadow you in death.' We both laughed at that, but soon got back to the awful reality of poor Barry lying there, chest rising and falling with each breath. In the end I decided, with Sally's approval, to do the interview and hope he was alive when I returned home. The truth was, it would make no difference to him if he died when I wasn't there.

I'd booked a hotel near Broadcasting House for the night and in the morning promoted my memoir on the show, alongside fellow guests Fay Weldon, cartographer John Hessler and actor Ed Zephyr. Libby asked about its title, *No Way But Gentlenesse*, and I explained it was taken from Edmund Bert's *An Approved Treatise of Hawkes and Hawking*, in which he'd written in 1619: 'There is no way but gentlenesse to redeem a hawk'. She then asked me to read a passage from my own book, encapsulating why I felt so passionate about hawks myself. I chose this:

> Kes had been born in the wild, and one day in October 1965, I released her back to where she belonged. Or to use the falconry term, I'd decided to 'hack her back' to the wild. After I'd fed her on the glove, I cut off her leather jesses, raised my arm and she soared into the sky. That wasn't the last time I saw Kes, for the next day at the same time I was back in the field swinging the lure. She must have flown low across the field behind me, because I was only aware of her presence when she seemed to appear out of nowhere and snatched the lure and tried to fly off with it. She'd never done that before. Finally I threw the meat I'd been holding to the ground and she dropped the lure, grabbed the meat, and carried it to a fence post to eat. I was struck by how quickly she'd forgotten the lessons I'd taught her, how wild she'd become. Witnessing how quickly Kes had reverted to the wild brought home to me the appeal of hawks, why I was obsessed with them. They have no understanding of hierarchy, of social subservience, it's not in their make-

up to be herded and controlled. Shouting or bullying or using physical force won't make a hawk submissive. I loved their wildness, how they can't be domesticated, how their will can't be broken by cruelty or violence. One of my favourite quotes came from *The Goshawk*: 'The mishandled raptor chose to die.' Yet over my summer flying Kes, I'd shown how a hawk's intractable nature can be won over. I loved the advice given by Nicholas Cox in his 1674 *The Gentlemen's Recreation*: 'You must by kindness make her gentle and familiar with you.' I think it was this wisdom, passed down from earlier centuries, which made hawks so appealing to me, this insight that an intransigent hawk, whose wildness is never lost and always resides just beneath the surface, can be reached, not by force, but by gentleness and kindness. It intrigued and delighted me that by treating Kes kindly while keeping my side of the bargain to provide her food and fly her free in the fields, I'd been allowed to spend a summer and autumn in her presence.'

I was honoured to be on the programme alongside legendary brilliant feminist author Fay in particular. In the studio, we all sat around a table as Libby chatted to us before going on air. The chairs had wheels and as we stood up Fay's chair ran backwards. She was about to fall and I ran behind it and caught her.

Through it all I remained in constant contact with Sally, who by now lectured in gender studies, and told her how I'd done my bit for feminism by preventing the great Fay Weldon from coming a cropper. Of course the real reason I'd rung was to check on my brother. She said his condition hadn't changed, still critically ill, and his son Tom was also driving up from his home in London. Next day, as Jackie and I drove through Wentworth and past the Hoober Stand, I was relieved Barry hadn't gone while I'd been away. Arriving at the care home, we sat with him in his room while Sally went out for a coffee.

As he lay there, eyes closed, breathing laboured, I told him it wouldn't be long before the martins and swallows arrived, then it would be the swifts, squealing up to their nest in the eaves of the houses in Queen Street and Sale Street on Hoyland Common. I was reminding him of our walks around Tankersley together when he opened his strikingly-pale blue eyes. With great effort he managed to raise his shoulders off the bed and, eyes fixed on my face, opened his mouth, trying to speak. The words wouldn't come, though, and he fell back on to the bed and closed his eyes. Next morning when Jackie and I returned, tapped in the code on the lock and walked through a door, a carer came out of the office and told us that Barry had died.

My brother's funeral was held in Tankersley Church on Tuesday 4 April 2016, a sunny afternoon. His son and daughter, Sally and Tom, together with Jackie, myself and the rest of his family, walked behind the hearse to the church where wild yellow primroses flowered between gravestones. When the six bearers heaved his coffin on to their shoulders and carried it through the lychgate we were joined by *Kes* producer Tony Garnett, director Ken Loach and actor David Bradley, aka Billy Casper, walking along the path to the accompaniment of music from the film, speakers set up especially for the occasion. Inside, the pews were packed with extra chairs set up at the back. Hymns were sung and prayers said until the time arrived when it was my turn to stand at a lectern and speak via a microphone into a sea of faces.

I spoke of being proud of Barry when I was ten and he'd been seventeen, a Teddy Boy in a fingertip-length jacket and narrow legged trousers. I thought he looked great dressed up in his suits, with those striking eyes of his and brushed-back fair hair. And how once when I saw him jiving with his girlfriend at a local dance, I'd thought he looked dead cool.

I went on to say he wasn't only a good dancer, but also a good footballer who played for England Grammar Schools. And how I'd answered a knock on the door one day to see a man in an overcoat and trilby who turned out to be a Manchester United

Richard in front of the ruins of Tankerley Old Hall in 2016

scout here to offer him a trial. And then of how my pride had turned to disappointment when he turned down the offer of a trial because he wanted to become a PE teacher.

I then spoke about the summer he was working on his novel, *A Kestrel for a Knave*, and preparing to write countryside scenes. And how on our walks we would wade through tall grasses in meadows full of ox-eye daises, yarrow and purple vetch, and how if we came across something we didn't recognise, Barry would pick a single flower or a stalk of grass and carefully put it in his pocket for identification when he got home.

I ended by saying I was still proud of Barry and admired the way his books gave a voice to working-class people.

Sally was next to rise from those dark oak pews and stand at the lectern where, with tears in her eyes, she remembered happy times spent with her dad. She, a university professor, spoke of how Barry supported her when she'd abandoned her A-Levels to live at the women's camp, telling her she could always come back to studying. Then she made us laugh when she told us how, after she'd been arrested for trying to climb the fence at Greenham, her dad visited her in prison and complained he'd had to miss a Sheffield United match. She then introduced Barry's favourite song. I budged up so she could rejoin me on the pew and we smiled as 'Teenage Kicks' by The Undertones blasted out.

Tony Garnett was next up and, as he spoke about Barry's authenticity as a writer and a man, he kept glancing at the coffin on trestles nearby, as if he was trying to come to terms with the reality that his friend of many years would no longer be around.

Ken Loach came to the lectern and paid tribute, pointing out that while Barry was a very good writer with an eye for comic detail, what had made *A Kestrel for a Knave* and his other works stand the test of time were their political themes and humanity.

Service over, Reverend Hale asked if anyone had anything else they would like to say. One man, reminded by what Ken had said about Barry's humour, made us all laugh in recalling a scene from Barry's novel *The Gamekeeper*, where the lord of an aristocratic estate has come across a poacher on his land and tells him: 'My ancestors fought for this land.' To which the poacher replies: 'Take thi coat off and I'll fight thee for it.'

Then a man ran down the aisle and stood at the lectern. He told us Barry had taught him in a Barnsley secondary school. He read a poem which praised Barry for being an inspirational teacher. This turned out to be Ronnie Steele, a local poet.

After the burial in the churchyard Sally stopped and gazed at the spire of St Peter's Church beyond Hoyland Common, then said, 'That's where Grandma and Grandad Hines are buried.'

I don't know if Sally felt the same as I did, but her saying that gave me a comforting sense of belonging to this landscape where my family and ancestors had lived and died.

20.

A FEW WEEKS AFTER BARRY'S FUNERAL, I visited his grave at Tankersley Church, then followed the path to my stepdad Bob's grave beside the moss-covered stonewall.

It was a warm sunny day, the wild yellow primroses were still in flower between the gravestones. Now sitting on the wooden bench beside the church, I remembered how over a decade ago, Jackie's mother, who had known Bob since they were children living in Wentworth, rang to tell us he had turned up at her house dressed in his usual highly-polished brown shoes, a sports jacket, a pair of garden gloves and a neatly-knotted tie over a striped pyjama jacket. I couldn't help laughing, but did wonder if he had early signs of dementia.

I was his stepson. Although his son Stuart had died years ago, while he was married to my mother, he had other blood relatives; a grandson, daughter-in-law, brother, sister-in-law and niece. Jackie and I were both working and had enough on our plates looking after her eighty-odd year old mother, so I'd felt if he did need help and care it was up to his own family to arrange it.

Walking down the drive after my mother's death, Jackie and I would often stand and admire the back garden of her and Bob's house, which he still lived in for a while; borders full of flowers, freshly-mowed lawn. He was always out when we called, though. Once, wondering if he hadn't heard me knock, I looked through a dining room window to see if he was in. In contrast to outside, the room was a mess. The table, sideboard, top of the television and chairs were piled high with envelopes and parcels of all sizes, as was most of the carpet. The next time we called and peered through, even more post cluttered up every flat surface.

I'd no idea why Bob's dining room was stacked with mail but felt it was none of my business. But when my cousin Pete, who lived in Hoyland Common, rang to tell us he'd seen Bob in the post office arguing with the postmaster, who was explaining to him he'd already been paid his weekly pension earlier in the day, I realised he needed help. It turned out his family couldn't cope after all and so I ended up looking after him.

One day, I sat at the dining room table surrounded by black plastic sacks full of junk mail, mostly begging letters or promises of fortunes – if Bob would first send a cheque. Others were from spiritualists who, for a fee, would put him in touch with his beloved dead wife. He tried to stop me binning one of these, saying she was a kind woman to whom he had posted cheques before. The only time he had rung me was to say excitedly that he'd won millions on a lottery but needed to send a cheque before they could pay him out. And as with the spiritualists, he became upset when I told him these people were criminals and not to be trusted. While I was sorting it all out he answered the telephone. I took it off him and asked who was calling. 'A friend of Bob's,' said a friendly voice. But when I said I was his stepson and asked what he wanted, he hung up. I think this was the man in Canada to whom he had posted a thousand-pound cheque. He had also posted another six hundred pounds to Japan.

I felt angry flicking through the stubs in his cheque book and checked his bank account. Poor trusting Bob, nearly 90 years of age, had been duped out of thousands. Some of his donations that had been repeated often were touching; donkey sanctuaries, cats' homes, animal rescue centres and such. But many of the cheques, ranging between a hundred and a thousand pounds, were now in the bank accounts of criminals who bought mailing lists of addresses and phone numbers of vulnerable old people.

Bob would occasionally say, 'I'm not without money,' which I found touching as I knew most of his life-savings, along with money from the sale of Mother's house, had been stolen. All he had was his state and small private works pensions.

I contacted the doctors and took Bob to Barnsley Hospital for tests. In one, he was asked to remember words in the order the doctor showed him on a printed card. In another, asked to write a sentence, he took a fountain pen from his pocket, bent over the desk and, in neat handwriting in royal blue ink, wrote one that made perfect sense. On the day I took him there he was smartly dressed, articulate and polite. It was difficult to believe he had Alzheimer's but he had. I arranged for carers to call in every day.

Bob still had a few hundred pounds of savings left, so through a solicitor I handed over managing his finances to a government body, who I had to contact for approval if I needed money to care for him. Such as the time I had to pay to disconnect the gas so he didn't blow himself up, along with John and Lydia who lived in the adjoining semi. Another time, when his feet were swollen, I asked for money to buy him a new pair of shoes with leather straps and Velcro to fasten them, rather than laces. He refused to wear them and, using a small shiny metal shoehorn, continued to squeeze his feet into his highly polished lace-up brown ones.

One day, after I'd taken him shopping, I walked through the door at home in Sheffield and the phone rang. It was Bob asking me to drive back to Hoyland Common because we'd forgotten to buy prunes for his breakfast. One Saturday morning Jackie and I were looking forward to a walk on the moors up the road, hoping to hear the sad burbling song of the curlew and forlorn call of the golden plover, when it rang again. It was Bob's carer this time. She told me he was sitting at the dining room table and wouldn't let her in the house. I rang him and when he answered he said: 'There's a woman looking through the window while I'm having my breakfast.'

'Let her in Bob,' I said. 'It's your carer.'

'I'm not letting her in,' he said, and hung up.

Twenty minutes later I walked down the drive and saw at least ten people standing outside the dining room window. The carer had called a friend, as well as her dad and his mate, who was a handyman who could take a door off its hinges if needed. A few neighbours had also come to see if they could help. Inside Bob was sitting at the table ignoring them. I asked them all to stand out of sight and knocked on the window. He saw it was me and unlocked the kitchen door to relieved laughter and cheers.

Before he became ill with Alzheimer's, he told me about the only time he had got drunk. It was on 30 September 1938, when Prime Minister Neville Chamberlain had strode down the steps of an aeroplane waving a piece of paper signed by Adolf Hitler and himself, claiming this agreement meant war between Britain and Germany had been averted. Bob went into The Rockingham Arms in Wentworth to celebrate and overdid it. It was so out of character. The sight of him staggering and swaying his way home through the village caused much laughter; it took days for him to live that one down.

Hitler didn't keep his promise. Germany invaded Poland, and Britain and France declared war. In 1939, at the beginning of the World War II, Bob volunteered to become an aircraft mechanic in the Royal Air Force and was stationed in Blackpool. He told me he'd wanted to marry Hilda, his first wife, in Tankersley Church. His senior officer was sympathetic but said he couldn't allow time off to go to Tankersley, but paid for Hilda to come to come and marry him at the seaside, with a two-day honeymoon.

The RAF billeted Bob and the other volunteers in a boarding house and each morning, rather than being woken by a sergeant major army type, as I'd imagined, the RAF equivalent of that rank walked the corridors singing: 'Good morning... Good morning...'

Bob began his aircraft mechanic training in a high-rise car park. Like all trainees, he began on the top level. Then, as his competence improved, he moved down to the next level to learn further skills and so on. Finally he reached ground level, became qualified, and was sent to work on Spitfires and Hurricanes. I imagined Bob would have worked on fighter planes in a hangar, so was surprised when he said they were parked in an open field. He also told me that after repairing an engine he had to go on a test flight with the pilot to make sure the problem was sorted. He smiled when I said that must have made him concentrate on his job, but was silent for a few moments after telling me that many of the fighter pilots never made it back to the airfield.

It was the Spitfire and Hurricane pilots who beat the German Luftwaffe in the 'Battle of Britain' to thwart an expected invasion, leading to Winston Churchill's famous speech: 'Never in the field of human conflict was so much owed by so many to so few.' The Spitfire and Hurricane pilots were 'the few'. As a mechanic who serviced and repaired their engines to keep them flying, Bob had a role in this victory, but Alzheimer's stole it from him.

Except for one memory.

When I sat with him in his house in Tankersley Lane, Bob would hold his hands cupped together in a 'V' shape. I can't remember if the plane was a Hurricane or a Spitfire, but he said one engine was shaped like that and one day he had accidently dropped a screw into it. Not knowing how to get it out he'd asked a fellow mechanic for help. This man said he had the very tool for the job and took a bent metal coat hanger out of his tool bag. He then handed it to Bob, who used it to fish out the screw.

One day, I opened the kitchen door and he'd chiselled all the tiles off the wall and neatly stacked them on the draining board.

Another time, I was about to take him for a walk and he stood at the bottom of the stairs saying: 'I'll tell my wife I'm going out.'

'You've got a bit muddled up, Bob,' I said. 'She died.'

'I'll just check.'

Upstairs, I could hear him walking into the bedrooms calling: 'Annie ... Annie ... Annie.' When he came down, he looked over the bannister at me standing in the hall, smiled, and said, 'You were right – she's not there.'

On my next visit he told me he had something to show me and led me up the stairs. In the front bedroom, he looked at the bed and said, 'It's not there.'

'What's not there?' I asked.

'The baby.'

Pointing to a spot between the duvet and a pillow he said, 'It was there.'

'How long was it there?'

'Three days.'

'Did you feed it?'

'No.'

'Think about it, Bob,' I said. 'If you hadn't fed the baby it would have died and be there in the bed.'

After a few moments he said: 'Fair enough.'

Physically fit, Bob didn't need to take tablets or medicines and enjoyed walking every day. But on my next visit, a neighbour told me he had been wandering up and down Tankersley Lane knocking on doors to tell embarrassed and concerned neighbours he would like them to have the Bible he was carrying in his hand.

I could no longer ignore that he needed to be in a care home.

21.

AT HOME IN SHEFFIELD, I find a blue cardboard folder with 'Bob's documents' written on the front. Inside is a brochure for Wentworth Hall Residential Home.

On one page, beside a photograph of a man in a kilt playing bagpipes, the brochure tells us of an event held each year, 'Burns Night supper with a visiting piper'. Under the heading 'MEALS' is a photograph of a white-haired old woman with dangling ear-rings. She is wearing a paper party hat. This was her birthday, the brochure tells us, and she is about to eat a meal chosen herself as a special treat. Another photo shows an old lady with permed grey hair wearing a pink jumper and cardigan, seated at a table. Behind her, in white overalls and cap, stands a young woman who reaches over her shoulders to help her hold the handle of a frying pan containing a pancake they are about to toss together.

Momentarily, I am amused by the thought of myself as an old man becoming involved in such events, designed to jolly old folk along. Particularly the absurdity of sitting in South Yorkshire, England, on Burns Night, unfathomably listening to Scottish bagpipes. But then my heart began to ache.

It struck me that the women in these photographs were the mothers of concerned daughters and sons who suffered the same sadness I'd felt when I first read the brochure, visited the place to check it out, and led Bob out of his home for the last time.

I still remember that day in September 2004 when I loaded two suitcases of his clothes and possessions into the boot. Then with him beside me and Jackie in the back, I drove to Wentworth, past fields of stubble where newly-cut wheat had been bundled into rectangular bales. The swifts had left *their* homes weeks earlier, but the swallows and martins had yet to go and flew over the village as we turned up to the church and parked outside Wentworth Hall Residential Care Home.

Built of a creamy coloured sandstone, the converted Victorian vicarage had tall chimneys and a large arched window on the second floor. Below this was an arched oak door. Bob, slim and handsome, his grey hair combed back, was smartly dressed in a jacket, shirt and tie, grey trousers and polished shoes. He looked like a retired public school educated army officer. Always the gentlemen, he greeted the matron politely when she opened the door and followed her up the staircase as she gave us a run down on meal times and routines, showed us his room, then said she'd leave us to settle him in.

Unsure what to do, he stood in the middle of the room as I told him he now lived in Wentworth village in the Rectory, where he used to come as a boy when preparing for confirmation at church. Pointing to a window, I told him that beyond those trees was the house in which he was born. As I assured him he'd soon settle, I saw Jackie had tears in her eyes as she hung his clothes in a wardrobe.

I would visit him later in the week and, after we'd called to see Jackie's mother at the weekend, we'd visit him together.

In those first few weeks we found him on the veranda looking confused, lonely and lost. Yet when we took him to walk his old haunts in the village, although he couldn't remember what had happened minutes earlier, memories of his childhood came back to him.

One day, walking past the red-brick boys' school where he had been a pupil before going to grammar school, Bob laughed as he recalled how one morning the headmaster had entered the classroom accompanied by the manager of the Co-op, still in his white smock. Holding up a piece of paper, the headmaster said someone had pushed this through the shop's letter box last night, then read out the hand written message: 'We're going to rob you buggers.' Silencing any laughter, he asked the boys if they knew who had written it.

'No, sir,' the boys answered in unison.

They were then ordered to take out their handwriting books and put them open on the desk. Walking up the aisles, comparing the handwriting on the piece of paper with that in the books, it wasn't long before the headmaster stopped beside a desk and led a blushing boy out of the classroom to his office.

Another time, when we were passing his boyhood house on Back Lane, Bob remembered the day when, aged ten, he got his first bike and chuckled as he said it was a girl's one without a cross-bar that had belonged to one of the Fitzwilliam daughters. She'd told Bob's dad she was getting a new bike and selling the old one so he asked the Countess if he could buy it for Bob and Bert, his sons. She said he didn't need to and later that day Lord Peter, who was to become the next Earl, five years older than Bob, rode down the Lane and delivered it to their house. He then held the saddle to help them balance while they took it in turns to ride it.

This sparked another story. One day, standing up peddling with Bert on the seat, they were stopped by a policeman. The local bobby was on holiday and instead of the fatherly telling off they would have expected, they were fined. When the Wentworth bobby returned he was dismayed to see the two summonses in the police station waiting to be delivered. It seemed this town bobby from Rotherham didn't know that in Wentworth village, cases for the magistrate were poaching or robbery, or other serious crimes. Not for lads riding two on a bike, especially when those boys were the sons of the butler. This local bobby was embarrassed and did not want to start rumours by being seen delivering the summonses to their front door. So, instead of knocking, he waited until it was dark before he walked up a path behind the house and knocked on the back door to deliver them.

Pheasants and red-legged partridges were reared by game-keepers on the Wentworth Estate, released to be shot in autumn. One day on our walk around the village I pointed out a covey of the latter pecking in the stubble fields. That reminded Bob of the time his dad told Lady Fitzwilliam that partridges and pheasants were eating seeds and plants in his garden and she'd given him a gun. 'Shoot them,' she had told him, 'and ask your wife to cook them for dinner.'

Whenever I visited we would walk out of the old Rectory grounds, turn left, then turn left again when reaching the church with its towering spire and walk on along Back Lane. I always pointed to the window of the stone house in which Bob was born when his dad was under-butler to Earl Fitzwilliam in 1915. He hadn't anything to say about living there; perhaps he'd left while very young. But when we stood outside 'The Laurels', the larger house they'd moved to when his dad became head butler, and where he'd lived as a boy and young man, he said it had always been his brother's job to cut the beech hedge out front.

His job as a lad was to fetch the family's milk. Pointing to a gate beside the hedge, he told how each morning he'd open that gate and, jug in hand, walk down the lane past cawing rooks in the rookery, cross the road, go through a green-painted door in the high sandstone wall and then into the estate dairy. The dairy maid would fill his jug then return to making cheese. Laughing, he told me how one morning, after having his jug filled, he'd been left alone. Curious to see how the cheese-maker machine worked he turned a tap and flooded the dairy with the stuff, so scarpered.

Another day as we looked across the fields, I reminded Bob how this had all been parkland until Clement Attlee's Labour government nationalised the coal industry and, in 1946, Manny Shinwell, minister for fuel and power, ordered that Wentworth Estate had to be open-cast mined at a time of coal shortages. I went on to remind Bob how trees were felled and the landscape disfigured by diggers with caterpillar tracks filling their buckets from the Barnsley seam outcrop a few feet beneath the grass on which red deer had grazed for centuries.

The plan to dig for coal there outraged the locals and the miners. Peter Fitzwilliam, who had taught Bob to ride a bike, was now the eighth Earl Fitzwilliam. His father the seventh Earl, who had died three years earlier, had established their reputation as good employers in the pits; miners and their families welcome to walk on estate land. Not wanting this beautiful landscape to be destroyed, the miners came up with a plan to extract the coal from a drift mine: the pit head would be outside Wentworth Park and have a sloping shaft which the men would walk down, and the coal would be brought on conveyor belts to the surface. Joe Hall, leader of the Yorkshire Area branch of the National Union, wrote to Prime Minister Attlee in support of the plan. But Manny Shinwell, a Glaswegian on the left of the Labour Party, was having none of it and the large caterpillar tracked diggers trundled in.

Lady Mabel Fitzwilliam, sister of the seventh Earl Fitzwilliam, was a Labour Party member and local councillor. I suggested to Bob that, despite this, I thought she would have supported the local miners rather than the government on the estate she had known as a child and young woman before marriage. Lady Mabel, a Christian socialist, said of her brother: 'He had so much and everyone else so little.' Her niece called her auntie a rabid socialist. I wish I'd thought to tell Bob this. I can image his response. Smiling, he would have said, 'Like your mother.'

He told me that for a shilling a year the estate workers and their families could play tennis on the courts next to the church, or cricket on the pitch in front of the Big House, or golf. The golf course was no longer there, but one day Bob pointed out where its different greens had been. I knew he had been a good player and he laughed again as he told me Earl Fitzwilliam was hopeless. He'd seen him fling a putter or similar through the air and order his professional coach to 'Burn all my bloody clubs.'

I've no idea of course, but I wondered if something Bob told me contributed to the Earl's bad mood. While young he overhead his dad telling his mother that Lady Fitzwilliam's friendship with a famous classical music conductor, who had a reputation for affairs with aristocratic ladies, could cause a scandal. He grinned as he told me of his dad's intense dislike of this chap and how he fumed at how he and Lady Fitzwilliam spent so much time alone while he sat in the corridor until the early hours, waiting for the bell to summon him again to carry in his silver tray of drinks.

I enjoyed our walks, listening to the stories that came back to Bob and seeing him relaxed and smiling. But as we made our way back through the village his mood would change. Walking up towards the church I could sense his feeling of dread when we stopped outside the care home. The ritual was always the same. He'd look towards Back Lane and say: 'I'll just walk up and see my mother.'

'Bob, you're nearly 90,' I'd say. 'She'd be about 120. She died a long time ago.'

'Fair enough,' he would reply.

22.

WHEN IT RAINED AND WE didn't go for a walk, Bob and I sat in two of the high-backed chairs set out around the walls of the care home lounge. Without the sights, sounds, landmarks and landscape of the past as a reminder his memory deserted him.

I have in front of me a book I made which we'd look through together when I visited in poor weather, and that I hoped would remind him of his family and history. One page has a photograph of 12-year-old Bob in 1927, standing with his mother and brother, Bert. Others show him with his first wife Hilda; some are of his son, Stuart, and grandson, Alexander. On another page I've typed: 'You married your second wife – Annie – in 1973.'

Below it are two photos of their wedding. One shows Bob and Mother standing in front of Tankersley Church's arched stone doorway, him in a dark suit with a white carnation pinned on his lapel, her in a dark blue outfit, white hat and gloves, clutching a small black handbag. In the other, they are both smiling as Bob prepares to cut the two-tiered wedding cake.

On one visit, as I sat in the lounge with him looking at these photos of him as a boy in Wentworth, a woman next to us joined in and told us she was Mrs Woodcock, who used to live at Manor

Farm on Main Street. We both listened as she told us about the day a magnificent tree in full leaf looked as if it was going to be blown over, and how she feared it would destroy the farmhouse. The roaring wind did indeed topple the tree, she said. But instead of it crashing down as she'd expected, the twigs and branches cushioned its fall and it slowly toppled over, landing with a 'WHOOSH' and missing their home, except for the end of a branch which broke a kitchen window.

I hoped he had found someone who could share Wentworth memories with him but, instead, he struck up a friendship with Mary, an elegantly dressed woman who a carer said was a retired headmistress. Each time I visited I found her sitting with him on a sofa in the lounge and I'd pull up a chair and sit beside them.

One day, flicking through the book I made for him, I found a photograph of his old Peugeot car and showed him it. Before I could explain why I'd done this, Mary, who also had Alzheimer's, shot to her feet, turned to face him, grabbed his hands, dragged him up off the sofa on to his feet and shouted: 'Come on, Bob. Let's go outside and look at your car.'

Jumping up, I stood in front of them, blocking their way.

'Mary, sit down! Bob, sit down and listen!'

Once they'd settled back, I told him I'd sold his car to his next door neighbour, John, and gently reminded him he was too old to drive now and that John had paid a good price for it. He didn't speak; just sat there quietly.

A few weeks later, instead of pulling up my chair to sit beside them, I told Mary I needed to speak to Bob alone.

We found a quiet place on the veranda and I told him I'd had to sell his house to pay for his care. Looking at me, he said: 'So I'll never be able to go home again?'

I gently shook my head.

A tear rolled down his cheek.

***

Richard's mother and stepdad, Bob, on holiday in later life

A few weeks later poor old Bob, almost ninety and the only man in the care home, was kicked out for ungentlemanly behaviour: wandering the corridors at night and climbing into bed with the female residents.

When the Principal of the home called Jackie and me into her office and told us of her decision, we agreed it must have been frightening for the women. But I stuck up for Bob and said he'd wake up in the night, have no idea where he was, and wander the corridors, most likely looking for his wife. Then I asked if they could lock his door – his room had a bathroom – and have a care worker check in on him regularly throughout the night?

She dismissed this idea and Jackie and I glanced at each other bemused, as she said something about it being a Christian home, and that the home's owners expected her to make sure it had a Christian atmosphere. The Principal had made up her mind and made it clear that she wanted us to find another care home for lifelong church-going Bob. She suggested that a council-run one might be more suitable.

When I drove over to Wentworth to take him to his new care home in Hoyland, I found him sitting on the sofa with Mary, and she stood in the arched doorway of the old vicarage to wave him off. As we drove down the lane from the church I asked him: 'Will you miss her?'

'Who?'

'Mary.'

'Who's that?'

***

The managers and care workers at the brick built Royal Court Care Home were really friendly and the rooms were cosier than the high-ceiled bedrooms in the old Wentworth vicarage.

From Bob's, you could see Beacon Hill in Wentworth, where for centuries large bonfires had been lit to celebrate national events; coronations; victories in battles. But when I pointed this out to him and asked if he remembered seeing blazing beacons on the hilltop, he didn't seem interested. He seemed to be lost in his own world and, as he sat there, he would occasionally say, 'I wish they'd hurry up.' It seemed as if he felt he'd become trapped in a waiting room, forever listening for a call that never came.

23.

A FEW MONTHS LATER IN JANUARY 2005, our phone in Sheffield rang in the early hours of the morning. It was a carer from the Hoyland care home. Bob had died. I had known him almost twice as long as I had known my own father.

Mother had many friends. One kind couple, Mr and Mrs Birkinshaw, took her on holiday one year to Northern Ireland. I remember her showing me a photo of the Giant's Causeway in County Antrim. She was grateful but always the odd one out, the only widow in her married circle. Marrying Bob in 1973 – ten years after Dad's death – rescued her from lonely widowhood. Bob became a devoted husband and loving stepgrandad to our young children, John and Katie. They liked him, but it amused them how Grandma Hines bossed him about. If they were spending the day with her on a Sunday, she would bake onions in the oven which when peeled were really sweet. Katie and John loved them. One Sunday, when they were sitting in the back seat of Bob's car as they drove through Harley, a small village with a few shops, Grandma Hines suddenly shouted, 'Bob!'

'What?' he yelled, braking sharply, thinking he was about to crash.

'Onions,' she said, pointing to a greengrocer's that was open on a Sunday.

I am looking at a letter Bob wrote, dated 9 May 1994, ten months after the death of my mother. Handwritten, it's touching. I can imagine him, wearing a tie, fountain pen in hand, sitting at the dining room table to compose it:

> *Will you please have my body cremated and arrange for the release of the ashes to you for final disposal and have them buried at the top of the right hand side of the grave of BERNARD and CLARA SANDERSON, opposite those of my first wife Hilda who was their daughter. You will find the grave towards the bottom of the right hand path in the old part of Tankersley Church graveyard.*

The Hoyland Common undertakers Harry Cook and Son had buried Dad in 1963 and Mother in 1993, so I asked Harry's grandson, now running the business, to organise Bob's funeral. It was he who collected Bob's ashes from the crematorium. The grave-digger had dug a hole in the earth for them.

A couple of weeks after Bob's funeral, on a cold January day with a cloudless blue sky, I sit on the wooden bench outside the church waiting for Reverend Hale to arrive and carry out Bob's final wishes. While waiting, I remember how Reverend Hale had given Bob a good send off and how, with his hand gently resting on the coffin, he had spoken so fondly of him. I am very fond of Tankersley Church and feel a connection to it; Bob and Mother's wedding was held here. This is also the bench where Jackie and I sat on our first date. But more than that, the church's history, its solemn interior and the religious rituals and hymns of Bob's funeral service moved me, which is surprising because since my late teens I haven't been able to believe that a supernatural God created the world and everything in it.

The memorial to nine-year-old Ann Fanshawe in Tankersley Church

Today, through genetic sequencing, we know all of us, all species, share a common origin, and our species, humans, can be traced back to Africa around two hundred thousand years ago; our female ancestors through mitochondrial DNA, our male ancestors through the Y chromosome. We now know everyone who has ever lived, those who are alive today, and those yet to be born, are African or descended from an African. And astrophysicists have worked out how in the big bang, about 13.8 million years ago, our universe ballooned outwards and is still expanding.

I couldn't see how religion and science about our lives and the universe could be reconciled, until I read a book by the American theoretical physicist and mathematician Brian Greene. He thinks that judging religion by whether it gives us factual information about objective reality is not the right way to judge it. Religion, he says, gives a sense of community; gives comfort as we face our mortality; and is an important part of human culture. It is in all our histories, and its rituals stretch back over a thousand years at least and connect us to our ancestors.

I am brought out of my thoughts when Reverend Hale walks through the lychgate accompanied by a church warden. I stand up from the bench to greet them, then sit down again while they go into the church to change into ceremonial clothes and collect the ashes. Minutes later, we are assembled by the stone arched church doorway. The reverend is wearing a white surplice, the church warden a black cassock and holding aloft a ceremonial pole topped with a brass cross. In my arms, I am soon cradling a polished rectangular box containing Bob's remains.

Reading from a prayer book, Reverend Hale leads the way, followed by the warden and me walking behind. As our solemn procession progresses I was vividly aware I am participating in a ritual that has taken place in this ancient churchyard for a thousand years. On the grass between the gravestones snowdrops are in flower; beyond the lichen-covered stone wall the green shoots of winter wheat are a few inches high; and beyond that on the horizon I can see the spire of Wentworth Church, close to Friar's House, where Bob had been born 89 years ago in the bedroom overlooking Back Lane.

24.

IN THE SUMMER OF 2016, I parked our car in Kirk Balk Cemetery beside a pine tree with fir cones scattered on the grass beneath it. Having visited Mother and Dad's grave, I stopped to admire the dahlias, tulips and roses on the grave of Keith Beaumont. Keith had lived a few doors up from us and had died in his early sixties, in 2009. I attended his funeral and the wake that was held in Hoyland Common Working Men's Club.

The last time I saw Keith was October 2004 in the club, where I'd gone for a Sunday lunchtime drink with Budgie, my lifelong friend. Keith was two years younger than us and Budgie ribbed him about the time as a lad he'd waded into a patch of long grass near the newt pond, then, suddenly high-stepping and lifting his knees as high as he could, ran back to Budgie and me screaming and crying because he'd seen a snake slithering through the grass and feared there might be others.

Keith had a sandy smooth-haired mongrel called Brownie. When I asked about Brownie he'd told me the dog had lived to a ripe old age. The conversation then turned to dogs we'd known as lads. I made them laugh when I reminded them of Charlie Whitworth's dog, Bodger, and how each time I took a short cut across derelict land to climb over the wall to get to our house, Bodger, barking crazily, would run out of Charlie's back yard to attack me. I'd let him get a few yards away then bend down and touch the ground as if about to pick up a stone to throw at him. Bodger never cottoned on. His haunches would drop to the ground and, straight front legs sticking out, he'd screech to a halt like a cartoon dog, turn tail, and run back into Charlie's yard.

Budgie reminded us of the large white chow that used to sit on the doorstep of Charlie Whitworth's neighbour and never seemed to move. Once, one of the comics, it could have been *The Dandy* or *The Beano*, had a Halloween mask inside every copy. Wondering if this chow was placid whatever the circumstances, Budgie devised an experiment. He walked up to it, stroked it as it sat calmly on the doorstep, then pulled the mask on, holding his face a few inches in front of the dog's. The chow curled its lip to reveal blue lips and gums and massive teeth and began to growl. Budgie backed off but, in his panic, forgot to take off the mask and the dog, snarling, edged closer, ready to attack. Budgie turned and, still wearing the mask, ran down Queen Street as fast as his legs would carry him with the chow giving chase.

Later, Keith joined some other friends while Budgie and me drank up and stood on the pavement outside the club chatting. When it was time to say goodbye he held my gaze as it hit us both that this could be the last time we ever went for a drink together.

A few months earlier, I'd driven over to Hoyland Common and just parked my car when I heard someone call 'Richard!' A woman walked across the road and asked if I'd heard the news about Budgie. For a moment, I'd thought he'd been killed.

After the closure of Rockingham Colliery he'd had another dangerous job, fixing corrugated sheets to the roofs of industrial buildings at a time when safety standards were lax. One evening when he joined me in the Prince of Wales on Hoyland Common there were no friendly greetings, no asking if I wanted another drink. He told me how, that afternoon, he and three workmates had been standing on a platform sixty or seventy feet high. They were chatting together, everything going well; it wouldn't be long before they finished for the day. Until out of the corner of his eye he saw one of his workmates overbalance and instinctively grab the workmate beside him in an attempt to save himself. Both fell over the edge. Budgie had watched, as if in slow motion, as they silently fell to their deaths on the factory floor below.

The woman who'd asked if I'd heard the news about Budgie told me he had cancer.

I wasn't expecting that. He was so fit and strong. Only a few weeks earlier he'd driven me and another friend, Baz, for a drink in a pub in a nearby village. When we came out his van had a flat tyre. Budgie took the spare wheel out of the back of the van, gave it to Baz, and then handed me a spanner. I expected him to take out a jack, but he closed the back doors and walked around to the driver's side where, pressing his back against the door, he held his arms straight by his side, bent his knees and gripped the sill beneath it. Then, with a mighty heave, he straightened his legs and lifted the van a few feet above the ground. I handed Baz the spanner and he changed the wheel. Baz was a mechanic, but it still took a few minutes. As the strain of holding the weight began to show on Budgie's face, he grinned at me and said: 'Go and get me a neck brace.'

After I'd heard the news of his illness I drove up to his house, parked the car, walked up the drive to his back door, knocked, and waited. At the bottom of the garden I could see flashes of colour – red, white, orange – as his beloved zebra finches flew between the perches of the aviary he had built. And I was struck by the brilliant blueness of the trailing lobelia, which cascaded down from the hanging baskets he had grown from seed in spring and hung on the garden shed. Budgie opened the door, and guessing what I was there for by the look on my face said: 'Has tha come to see if I've left thi owt in the will?'

We both laughed but were soon overcome by a sombre mood.

Queen's Silver Jubilee June 1977. Richard with Budgie, his wife Margaret, and their children, John, Thomas, and Kelly.

Inside he told me he'd thought his stomach pains could be indigestion, or at worst an ulcer, and that it hadn't crossed his mind it could be a 'tap dancer' – rhyming slang for a cancer. But it had been. Oesophageal.

He had a stent pipe fitted to keep his oesophagus open, which allowed him to eat and drink. He could still manage a couple of pints of beer, and I continued to drive over to Hoyland Common for a Sunday lunchtime drink. He hadn't lost his humour and his way of calling people to task who got above themselves. One afternoon, when we were in The Star at the top of Tinker Lane, a man we knew was boasting about a good deed he'd done. I don't recall why this man was so full of himself but I remember what Budgie said to him: 'There's a box of medals behind the bar, get thi sen one on thi way out.'

One day when I called in to see him he was putting away the lawnmower, having just cut the grass, and was about to take Meg, his chocolate coloured labrador, on a walk around Tankersley.

He looked so fit I said I hoped there'd been a misdiagnosis and that he would be okay. He replied he didn't think so. But the next time I called in I learnt there was hope. He'd had an appointment at Sheffield Hallamshire Hospital and the surgeon had told him he was so fit that he'd be able to have an operation and there was a good chance the tumour in his oesophagus could be removed.

A couple of days before his operation I walked the two miles from our house to the hospital, then up several flights of stairs to the ward. When I pulled up a chair and sat beside his bed I was out of breath. He ribbed me for being so unfit. Pacing the ward in pyjamas was a slim man in his fifties. Budgie told me the man was a cyclist, who each day until recently had ridden over the Derbyshire moors a few miles south of the hospital.

'Poor bloke,' I said.

'I know what he feels like,' Budgie said. 'But he's driving me bloody crackers.'

'Why?'

'Each time I close the curtains to get away from his pacing about, or to have a sleep, there it is. His face. Peeping through the bloody curtains.'

I couldn't help but grin at the image of this, but Budgie wasn't amused.

'It's alright for thee,' he said. 'It's not thee laid here.'

He went on to tell me how the surgeon would have to remove a rib so he could get to the oesophagus to cut out the tumour. Before I left I told him to try not to worry; that the surgeon wouldn't be doing it if he didn't think it would be successful.

I was full of hope as I walked to the hospital to visit him after his operation. But when I pulled up a chair beside his bed I knew the operation had gone wrong. He looked devastated. He told me how the surgeon had come to his bedside after the operation to explain that when he opened him up, he'd seen the cancer had spread to his liver. The chemo hadn't worked, his cancer was terminal. And that he'd had to abandon the operation to remove the tumour and sew up the incision.

Even before the surgeon had spoken to him, he realised his last hope of being cured had gone. The moment he woke from the anaesthetic he'd pressed his hand on his side and was overcome with fear. The rib that needed to be removed so the tumour could be cut out of the oesophagus was still there. It was in that moment, in that split second, he told me, when he'd clamped his hand on his chest, that he knew he was dying.

I visited him often at home. By this time he was losing a lot of blood and had to go into hospital for regular transfusions before returning home again. One day, as he lay on the sofa in his and his wife Margaret's front room and I sat in a chair, we were reminiscing about old times when it seemed to hit him how that was all he had now – a past but no future. He began to cry. But moments later his crying turned to embarrassed laughter and he said: 'Bloody hell, Richard. I never thought I'd roar in front of thee.'

On another occasion I told him I'd never forget him. After his embarrassment at crying, I wondered if such tender talk between two working-class blokes would make him uncomfortable and I expected him to respond with one of his funny comments. But he smiled and said: 'That's nice.'

On one visit to see Budgie at home he said he'd walk to the car with me. As usual, when we stepped out of the back door I looked down the garden at his aviary, expecting to see flashes of red, white and orange, as his treasured zebra finches flitted from perch to perch. Today the aviary was empty.

'Where's thi birds?' I asked.

'Sold 'em,' he said.

As we walked together down the drive he told me how

upsetting it had been; giving up his life-long hobby; arranging the sale of his finches on the phone; catching them up in a net in the aviary... At that moment, glancing up and down the road I cut him off and asked: 'Where's mi car?', then added, 'Sorry, it's over there. What was tha saying?'

'It doesn't matter,' said Budgie.

As I was heading off, he called his usual friendly goodbye: 'Keep thi timber up.' It's an old mining farewell which means take care of yourself by setting your wooden pit props correctly.

Driving home through a green tunnel of overhanging rookery trees, my heart ached. He'd been telling me how he felt when he said goodbye to a part of his life he loved. And I interrupted him. Wondering where I'd parked my car.

Jackie had known Budgie since 1970, following my return home from college and our wedding in Barnsley Town Hall. We often met up with him and his wife Margaret in the Prince of Wales and had attended their wedding in the same place. Their son, Tom, was born around the same time as our son, John. Jackie was with me when I saw Budgie for the last time. He had to spend most of his time in bed now, or lying on the sofa, but he'd managed to walk to the back door to see us off. He and Jackie hugged each other, clinging together with tears in their eyes. Jackie stepped back and he looked at me and we held each other's gaze for a few moments, then I gave him a gentle pat on the shoulder and we left.

He would have appreciated that amid the grief and solemnity at his funeral, there had also been laughter from the mourners packed on the pews – and those standing at the back unable to find a seat – when the priest reminded us that as a young man Budgie had been a poacher. Sometimes I accompanied him and saw him spread the nets over the burrows, slip a ferret under one of them, and watched the rabbits thundering out of their burrows into the trap. He always gave me a couple to take home to skin and cook. In later years he had given up on poaching. He couldn't bear to do that anymore he'd told me, and kept a sweet little pet rabbit which he fed from his fingers.

In the past, folk who lived in our parish were buried in St Peter's. Later, the old churchyard across Law Hill from the church became the burial ground. I once went in there with Mother and stepped between the overgrown graves, unsuccessfully searching for the gravestone of her younger disabled sister who had died aged six. And who, in the words of Mother, had been a lovely lass who was always smiling. My Grandad and Grandma Hines and their family, who had gone to seek work in Lister's cotton mill, are buried in Bradford. But my great grandad, John Hines, who drove a steam engine shunting wagons of coal in Rockingham Colliery pit yard, and his wife Sophia, are both buried in the old churchyard.

In the 1930s, Kirk Balk Cemetery became the place where people from our parish were buried. Budgie, as a lad, had lived in Queen Street just around the corner from me in Tinker Lane. Then he'd lived in Springfield Crescent and Springfield Road after he married his beloved Margaret. After his death he didn't want her to be forever traipsing up Law Hill with a bunch of flowers for the grave and so chose to be cremated.

Budgie and Margaret, who worked for the civil service, enjoyed travelling abroad: Europe, America, India. When he became ill and it looked as if a planned holiday would need to be cancelled I commiserated with him. But he told me he didn't care if he never went abroad again. And that he just wanted to get better, drive up Tankersley Lane with his labrador Meg sitting on the front seat of the van beside him, park at Tankersley Church and take her for a walk along the path beside the Bullwood.

25.

ONE DAY, SITTING AT HOME, I remembered the time I visited Budgie when he was terminally ill and he opened a drawer and handed me a pamphlet.

'I'd like thee to have this,' he told me.

He didn't elaborate why, but I guessed he wanted me to keep it as a reminder of a special day we spent together.

I've found it on the bookshelves and have it on the table in front of me. The white paper front cover has faded to a creamy colour and the print and illustration are in red ink.

Your Programme Number is – No 2246
ROCKINGHAM COLLIERY
CENTENARY
1975

Underneath is an illustration of pit winding gear and beside it a miner wearing a helmet with a lamp attached. And below:

OPEN DAY
31st March 1975
[Easter Monday]

The day I'd gone to the open day with Budgie is still vivid in my mind. For the first time, I experienced what it would have been like for Dad; entering the 'cage', a lift, then plunging hundreds of yards into the depths of the earth. Below ground, Budgie pulled aside sacking which signalled an out-of-bounds area, then took me on an unofficial tour along the dark tunnels. The very tunnels where Dad, aged 14, had ridden on the pit tub full of coal behind his pony, and held its reins as he'd glanced nervously at the shadows his miner's lamp had thrown on the walls. It was down here where Dad had knelt in a low seam and shovelled sixteen tons of coal a day.

In the programme, A. Parish, a local historian, had written a short history of the colliery and I was struck by this paragraph:

> *Except for a stormy interlude in the 1893 lock-out, when nearly 4,000 rioters set the stables on fire, wrecked the offices and lamp room, smashed up and set fire to waggons in the sidings, the subsequent history of the pit has been, on the whole, fairly successful.*

There is something about that sentence that made Budgie and me laugh. It might have been the vivid description of the violence being followed by the faintly damning, '*the subsequent history of the pit has been, on the whole, fairly successful.*' Whatever it was, it amused us and also made us both curious to know what events had caused such mayhem. Budgie asked me to try and find out about the history of the 1893 lock-out before he died.

Or as he put it: 'Try and find out about that lock-out will tha? While I'm still here?'

At that time, in early 2005, I was extremely busy teaching television and film screenwriting at Sheffield Hallam University. Today, it has taken me a while to find the programme on the bookshelf. It was wedged between several pamphlets about the history of Tankersley Church that were pressed against Arthur

Clayton's history of Hoyland, with its yellow cardboard cover and sticky-taped spine. Returning the open-day programme to its original place I am struck by an awful thought. I'd never checked to see if Arthur had written an account of the Rockingham pit lock-out. I flick through the photocopied stapled-together pages and find the chapter heading, *The Great Century of Coal.* And there on page seventy is an account of the Rockingham Colliery riot. Had I not been so tied-up with work I could have reached out from my favourite blue armchair, taken Arthur's book off the bookshelf beside me, and told Budgie about the riot he'd asked me to find out about before he died.

Arthur's account reminded me of some old photographs of Hoyland Common that used to be on our staircase but which, after decorating, we never rehung. I've retrieved them from storage in the cellar and can follow the route the rioters took on their way to the pit. The irony is, had I found out about the lock-out while Budgie was alive, I wouldn't have needed to drive over to Hoyland Common with my pictures. He could have followed the rioters' progress through our pit village himself on the identical photos he had on his wall at home. In the early 1980s, I'd been commissioned by Channel 4 to make a series of oral history programmes about working class life. While researching old photographs to use in that series I came across the three of Hoyland Common and had prints made for Budgie and myself. Looking at them on the table before me I dearly wish I'd read up about the 1893 incident when Budgie asked me to. Had I done so, I can imagine the scene after telling him what I'd found. He'd have taken his copies off his living room wall and, while we sat on the sofa looking at them, I imagine he'd have said: 'Thanks for doing this. I'm dead interested in finding out what happened.'

I would have told him we can follow the rioters' route through the village on the photos, but first he'd need to know why seven hundred miners had marched down Hoyland Road on their way to cause mayhem at our local pit.

'The Great Yorkshire Lock-Out of 1893', or the 'Ninety Three Strike' as it became known, was sparked by the mine owners.

Coal prices had fallen and to protect their profits owners throughout Yorkshire imposed a twenty five per cent pay cut on wages. Fearing they wouldn't be able to afford to pay their rent and buy food for their families, the miners, supported by the recently formed Miners' Federation, went on strike, demanding the owners pay them 'a living wage' – the phrase used at the time. The owners of Rockingham Colliery, the Newton Chambers Company, like all owners in the county, 'locked out' the miners from their collieries, preventing them from earning a living unless they agreed to abandon the strike and accept their wages being cut by a quarter. The miners refused.

Five weeks into the strike, on Tuesday 5 September 1893 in the nearby village of Wombwell, an official from the Miners' Federation was addressing around two thousand miners in the marketplace. Some of the men worked at Rockingham Colliery, many of the assembled were from other south Yorkshire pits. The union man's speech was interrupted when a messenger arrived with news that strike-breakers were loading coal into waggons from the stockpiles in the pit yards at Hoyland Silkstone Colliery in the village of Platt's Common, and at Rockingham Colliery. Both pits were owned by the Newton Chambers Company and the coal was being transported to Thorncliffe ironworks, which they also owned. This was black-legging. The furious strikers ignored the pleas of the Miners' Federation official urging them to keep calm and a crowd of around seven hundred men and youths, along with some women, decided to confront the strike-breakers. They swarmed out of the market square and headed towards Platt's Common, two miles away.

News of what was happening at the two Newton Chambers Company-owned collieries spread to other pit villages. When the seven hundred or so arrived at Hoyland Silkstone pit they were joined by hundreds more men, who descended on the pit yard from different directions. The strike-breakers who were loading the waggons from the stockpiles of coal fled, leaving the rioters to release the brakes on the waggons and send them careering down the track to crash off the rails. Windows were smashed in the room where the pit lamps were kept and the office buildings were ransacked. Books and papers were cast to the wind. When Mr Fincken, the colliery manager, pleaded with them to end their destruction he was hustled and pushed. Until workers from the pit who knew him yelled 'He's alright' and escorted him to safety.

Eventually, the thousand or more locked-out miners set off for Hoyland Common and the spire of St Peter's Church at the top of Law Hill, which could be seen on the skyline a mile away.

When this angry poverty-stricken ragtag army appeared over the brow of Law Hill, having plundered provisions from two horse-drawn carts, some were taking swigs from bottles of ginger beer, others eating sweets ... pear drops ... jelly babies ... some dipping liquorice sticks into sweet powdered sherbet. On hearing the raucous stream of strikers passing the church and heading down the hill, Reverend Sale, dressed in his ankle-length black cassock, hurried out of the St Peter's vicarage and walked among them. On hearing they were heading to the pit yard to confront the strike-breakers, he urged them 'return home'. In his account, Arthur Clayton says some strikers told Reverend Sale to mind his own business, others told him they needed to win their fight for a living wage to be able to feed their families and pay the rent. I have a photo of a family who were evicted in the 1893 lock-out. In it, a woman sits on a chair with her three children huddled up beside her, all staring at the camera. Behind them all the family's worldly possessions are stacked outside the backdoor; a scrubbed dining table, four wooden chairs, a sofa and an aspidistra.

The strikers were burning with indignant rage against the strike-breaking Rockingham pit top workers as they strode down Law Hill, past a stone farmhouse I knew as Hardy's farm and into Hoyland Common. Perhaps it was the farmer or his wife, or the

Richard, with his dog Flick, standing on the path leading to the wood where Budgie's ashes are spread – Tankersley Church in the background.

headmaster of the tiny 18th-century school a little further down Hoyland Road, but whoever it was they sent a boy running down it who breathlessly warned of the noisy shouting throng, setting off a panic throughout the village as shopkeepers shuttered their shops and teachers told schoolchildren to hurry home.

If Budgie and I had been sitting on his sofa together in 2005, we would now be looking at his copy of the photo of Hoyland Road taken in the late 1890s, or early 1900s. Heads poke out of attic windows above the shops. Below are women shop workers in white aprons and long black frocks, men in dark suits and flat caps, boys dressed in knickerbocker trousers like little old men, all gawping at the camera. In the distance it's possible to make out a group of 18th century stone cottages, now demolished. I would have pointed to the bend in the road in front of these cottages and told Budgie that's where the strikers must have first appeared on Hoyland Common.

The throng would have marched on down Hoyland Road and passed the stone-built boys' elementary school on their left. Pointing to the school, I'd have told Budgie how Dick Wilkinson, who we'd both known as a very old man, had as a boy stood on a chair and watched through a classroom window as the strikers streamed past. Grandad Hines would have been in school on that Tuesday in September 1893 and, knowing him, I guess he would also have found a vantage point to watch the rioters parading by. In elementary schools the year groups were called 'standards', and each year pupils had to pass an end-of-term exam before they could move up to the next level. Grandad used to joke: 'They'd have had to blow up the school to get me out of standard one.'

Later the boys' elementary school became a mixed boys' and girls' infant school. And on one September morning, fifty seven years later in 1950, Budgie and I, aged five, started school in the very classroom in which Dick Wilkinson had stood on a chair to watch the ragtag army of strikers pass by.

On the left edge of the photograph of Hoyland Road, beside the brick sidewall of a shop, is the entrance to Calvert Street where my grandad, who would also have seen the strikers pass the school, lived with his parents, my great-grandad Hines and great-grandma Sophia. The front room of their tiny terraced brick cottage was a workshop where, in his spare time, great-grandad made furniture to sell. He also cut up old clothes into 'clippings', then used a sharpened clothes peg to fix these into a piece of hessian to make patterned 'pegged' rugs, which he also sold. A heavy drinker, he used the extra money to buy whisky and beer. But his full-time job was driving a small steam engine that shunted coal around Rockingham pit yard. After I'd told Budgie this I can guess he would have said.

'Where was thi great-grandad when the rioters passed the end of their street? Pegging rugs? Or shifting coal in the pit yard to keep in with the bosses?'

And I would have had tell to him I didn't know, as no one in the family had ever talked about the lock-out.

In the second image, Allott's shop on the corner of Hoyland Road and Sheffield Road has legs of lamb hanging either side of the door frame. Standing between them, in a long white apron, the butcher gazes at the camera. A little further along Sheffield Road, the old turnpike, Allott's have a General Store. Displayed outside are wooden steps, a sweeping brush, boots and shoes tied together and hanging down in strings. A teenage girl in a white dress and black stockings is looking at the display. Further along the road, two women in ankle-length black dresses and straw boaters are walking together. But on that September day in 1893 when the fired-up locked-out miners marched around Allott's corner, the shop windows would have been shuttered, the doors locked and the streets would have emptied of residents.

The third photograph was taken further along Sheffield Road. Next to Hilton's Booteries is the Prince of Wales pub sign, with its three large feathers. From where I'm sitting, at home, I can see two tiles standing vertically, side by side on a shelf. The cream glazed tiles have a stylised design of a Lords and Ladies flower with green leaves and yellow petals. Had I found out about the lock-out as Budgie had asked, I'd have taken them over to his house when we looked at the photos and reminded him he'd chiselled them out of the entrance hall of the Prince of Wales for Jackie and me when they did it up, because we liked them. And added that they were on the wall when the rioters crowded through the door into the pub, demanding free ale, and that I liked the idea that great-grandad Hines's sleeve might have brushed those very tiles.

On the photo, the Hare and Hounds is a few yards further up Sheffield Road at the top of Queen Street. Trooping out of the pubs the rioters, now even more fired up with the alcohol they'd drank, would have passed the top of Regent Street and a row of stone houses and disappeared out of the edge of the photograph down Pit Lane.

In the pit yard, strike-breakers had been loading stockpiled coal into railway waggons to be sent to Thorncliffe Ironworks when news arrived that the Hoyland Silkstone rioters were on their way. Managers and officials told them to go home, then sent a message to the ironworks asking for help to quell the invaders. The reply said thirty-nine labourers were on their way.

News of the Silkstone riot had spread to other pit villages and boosted the numbers. At around quarter to one in the afternoon, three to four thousand angry men and women came marching down Pit Lane. The sight of them sent the managers and officials, along with the one policeman on duty, running across the yard to the engine house, where they barricaded themselves in. Still imagining we were looking at the photographs and talking about the pit riot, I'd have reminded Budgie how as lads we had sped through the pit yard on a flat-topped trolley the railwaymen used to check the lines, and jumped off at Dove Cliff. Then told him how the thirty nine blokes who'd been sent from Thorncliffe Iron Works to quell the riot had taken one look at the rampaging mob, and legged it down the side of that same track we'd rode down on the trolley, then jumped on a train as it pulled out of Dove station.

We'd have talked about the awful image of the shire horses that pulled waggons of coal in the pit yard galloping out of the burning stables, then realised they wouldn't have been in the stables. Instead, from the first day of the strike, the horses would have been out grazing in the fields with the pit ponies.

And of how, in the pit yard, a fanatical middle-aged man was inciting the rioters to wreck the offices ... and of how in the lamp room a woman called Mary Anne, from the village of Jump, threw a brick through a clock face ... and of how several others set fire to a couple of railway waggons in the sidings.

Six police constables arrived by train from Barnsley and made many arrests. Until a volley of stones, handed to the throwers by women who carried them in their aprons as ammunition, forced the police to release their prisoners and retreat. Later, in Barnsley police court, three of them were sentenced to three months each in Wakefield Prison. The riot, watched by thousands, went on for two hours. Most of the rioters, according to Arthur Clayton, weren't Rockingham miners because when the rioters left they went in different directions.

Except for a few bruises to the policemen caused by the stone throwing, no injuries were reported at Rockingham Colliery. But two days later, on September 7, there was a tragedy at Acton Hall Colliery in Featherstone. A large number of locked-out strikers were trying to stop stockpiled coal being loaded into waggons to be transported to Lister's mill in Bradford. The pit manager panicked and ran to the police station for help. On his way, by chance he met a local pit owner who recommended bringing in troops. When the army officer read the riot act and the angry crowd refused to disperse, the soldiers opened fire. Two miners were killed and sixteen wounded in a hail of bullets.

Concluding the story of this 'stormy interlude' in Rockingham pit's history, as local historian Alf Parish described it in his centenary pamphlet, I'd have told Budgie the strike ended sixteen weeks later on 7 November 1893. The government intervened and the mine owners, in a meeting with the union leaders, agreed the striking Yorkshiremen could go back to work on their old wages until a conciliation board was set up. The following year, the miners agreed to a ten per cent reduction in wages.

The trio of photographs of Hoyland Road and Sheffield Road in Hoyland Common, identical to those hanging on Budgie's wall, will be hung on a wall in our Hove flat. And the two tiles from the entrance hall of the Prince of Wales, which Budgie chiselled off the wall for Jackie and me, will also find a place on our new bookshelves there.

26.

ON THE DAY BUDGIE GAVE me the Rockingham Colliery centenary programme, he said: 'I've got something else for thi.' A couple of minutes later, he returned from his garden shed cradling something wrapped in a supermarket plastic bag and said, 'I want thee to have these. And if tha could, to try and find summat out about 'em while I'm still here.'

On the table in front of me I have what was in that bag: two dark brown solid oak wheels the size of dinner plates. Each wheel has a few cracks and knots and a two-inch hole drilled through the centre that would have held a wooden axle. They are from a small wooden coal truck that would have been pulled along a mine floor at a time before rail tracks.

After he left mining, Budgie worked for an opencast company and found these wheels in an old mine unearthed by the bucket of a digger. Unsure how to go about it and busy with work, I'd made no effort to look into its history but it turned out all I would have needed to do was check Arthur Clayton's Hoyland history. His hand-typed photocopied book doesn't have a list of chapter headings at the beginning or index at the end, but after randomly flicking through it, on page thirty nine I came across the chapter

'The Beginnings of Coal Mining' in which Arthur writes of how, in 1681, the Rokeby family were mining coal 'between the site of Hoyland Common and where Rockingham Colliery would be sunk two centuries later.' This was the mine where Budgie had found the wheels that are on the table in front of me.

I so wish I could ring and arrange to meet him. I'd love to have been able to walk our childhood haunts together and tell him what I'd found out, as we tried to work out the site of the mine where he'd found the wheels. Instead, fired up by reading Arthur's book, I'd driven over to Hoyland Common.

It was a warm sunny spring day with a cloudless blue sky. As I walked down the cart track, on the horizon I could see the spire of St Peter's. To my left, sparrows chittered somewhere in the fresh green leaves of elder and hawthorn. At the bottom of the track, a flock of starlings took flight in the field before me as I turned left beside the stagnant stream, its banks overgrown with bramble and grass. I would need to follow this stream to find the site of the mine that Budgie had said was below the large pond we called 'the Floods'. As I weaved and ducked through the silver birch and willow trees beside the stream I lost my bearings and, as on my previous visit, jumped across the stream and scrambled up a grassy bank. From here I could see the row of prefabricated houses in Tinker Lane and knew I was level with the end one. The old concrete bridge would have been where I was and the stream would have run for fifty yards into the Floods. I jumped back across the stream onto the other bank where, hanging on to the thin trunks of the saplings, I carefully paced out fifty large steps then stood still beside a pine tree. This was the very spot where the bucket of the opencast mining digger had unearthed the mine where Budgie found the wheels of the small coal truck.

When he worked at Rockingham pit, he told me how he'd occasionally split open a piece of coal and, in the light of his helmet lamp, could see a fossil of a fern or leaf. Standing deep underground, he would marvel at the thought that they had grown in a forest millions of years ago and he'd become the first person to see them. And he told me he'd had that same sense of wonder when the digger bucket lifted off the roof of the old mine.

The opencast mining firm he worked for had mined what was left of the 'outcrop' of Barnsley coal that the Rokeby family began to mine in the seventeenth century. An outcrop of coal is where a seam comes close to the surface. Sifting through a mass of documents preserved in the strong room of the Wentworth Estate, Arthur Clayton found a contract dated 23 September 1681. The Rokeby family granted William Coe the liberty of ingress (the right to enter the mine), egress (the right to leave the mine) and regress (the right to return to the mine and right to get and sell coal). Coe had to pay forty pounds rent a year and each year provide the Rokeby family with forty-three loads of coal. I had to smile at the contract stating he had the liberty to leave the mine; I'd have thought that wouldn't need spelling out.

For me the lease contract came to life after I'd read that Coe was not to employ more than four men to hew coal, and one to draw the coal up the pit, upon pain of one pound every day if he put in more than four. I'd had no idea how large the mine had been or how many men worked there. As I stood beside the pine tree on the site of the mine, in my mind's eye I could see a man; biceps bulging, face black with coal dust, as he heaved on a rope and pulled up a load. I could imagine the northern voices of the four hewers and the sound of their picks as they picked away at the coalface a few feet underground.

The lease stated only one mine could be open at a time and if the coal in it became exhausted the mine had to be filled in before another could be opened. This clause, along with allowing only four hewers to work in the pit, was to avoid too much damage to the landscape. From the site of the old mine, through the trees I could see fields stretching up to St Peter's on the top of the hill. In the seventeenth century this would have been common land; a patchwork of longfields and balks ploughed by teams of oxen and horses. As the farmers worked the land and occasionally stopped to watch the miners, the new tenants, I wonder if they felt a sense of apprehension, a stab of fear that the industry would bring changes they couldn't articulate but which would somehow threaten their way of life.

Wooden pit props used to support the roof in Rockingham pit when both my grandads, my dad and Budgie worked there, were made in saw mills. They were smooth and straight with a five-or-six-inch diameter – I'd seen piles of them in the pit yard waiting to be taken below ground. Budgie told me how, when the digger opened up the old mine, the first thing that fascinated and surprised him was that the props had been made by the miners themselves, using axes. The bark was still on the trunks of the small trees they had felled, and the branches had been lopped off leaving a few inches sticking out from the trunk. I'd have liked to tell him that reading Arthur's book I'd discovered the rough and ready roof supports he'd seen were called 'punchwood.'

Sifting through the documents in the Wentworth Estate strong room, Arthur had also come across the will of Thomas de Verigny, probably one of the Rokeby clan or a descendent. Whatever his connection, eighteen years after the mine had been sunk in 1681, when he died in 1699 he owned a mine on that site. Attached to his will was an inventory with the heading 'Coale Pitts', under which was a list of miners' tools.

First on the list was a firepan. I've no idea why they needed a pan of burning coals down a mine, but its inclusion in the list of tools suggests seventeenth century owners weren't aware of flammable gases down there and the catastrophic consequences of igniting them. A pick striking a rock can cause a spark; in later centuries faulty coal-cutting machinery or faulty fans did exactly that and caused explosions. In March 1875, as the pit shaft of Rockingham Colliery was being sunk, gas was ignited by the blasting and sent flames leaping into the sky. If relays of men hadn't pumped water into the shaft and put out the fire, our local colliery would not have existed. Throughout the eighteenth, nineteenth and twentieth centuries, there'd been numerous gas explosions in mines, sending fire raging through underground tunnels and bringing wives, mothers, sons, sisters and brothers running through the fields towards the leaping flames.

In Thomas de Verigny's 1699 will the full list of miners' tools reads: '*Fire pan, 10 Whole Picks & three broken ones, 7 Wedges, 2 Hammers, 5 Hurrying Hooks, 4 sleds, [trucks] 2 slipes, one Rake, one Hooke, 3 Pitt Ropes and 2 Hatchetts, all valued at a total of £1.*'

Knowing Budgie would be as confused about slipes as I was, I'd loved to have copied the tool list on to paper and, grinning, handed it to him saying: 'Tha knows when tha climbed down into the old mine to get them wheels? Did tha see two slipes?'

The wheels Budgie had found and given to me told the story of the origins of our village and its first miners. Reading Arthur Clayton's book I also found out how, in 1872, Lord Fitzwilliam had leased eight hundred acres to The Newton Chambers Company to deep mine on the site of the 1681 pit, and that our local one, Rockingham Colliery, was named for the first Marquis of Rockingham, an ancestor of the Fitzwilliam family. Once again, I so wished I'd done the research Budgie asked me for and was able to share this history with him. We could then have located the site of the old mine together.

Still standing beside the pine tree on the site of the 1681 mine, I came out of my thoughts, picked up a cone, put it in my fleece pocket and scrambled up the grass bank to the path. At the top of the cart track I stopped and looked out towards St Peter's. Occasionally, after visiting my parents' grave, I cross the road opposite the church on to a path that runs beside the graveyard in which my paternal grandparents are buried. From here I gaze down the hill at Hoyland Common village. Today, standing here, any stranger versed in the devestating consequences of burning coal to heat our homes and fuel the industrial revolution, and the urgent need to now use wind and solar power for our energy, would see below a village surrounded by countryside. They would have no idea this was a former mining village. Or that beneath the landscape of rye grass, birch and willow saplings, lay the pit yard and flattened slagheaps of Rockingham Colliery, and deep underground tunnels that stretched for miles and miles.

Rockingham closed in 1976 and it was Budgie who created an image that caught, for me, the lonely atmosphere of the pit's abandoned tunnels. Soon after its closure I was in the pub with Budgie and a couple of other miners. They were talking about an old man who was nearing retiring age called Sonny and saying what a beautiful singer he was. It was true. I'd heard him sing at funerals myself. Sonny was too old to work on the coalface and pressed the button that stopped and started the coal-carrying conveyer belt. It was cold work sitting there and he wore a large black overcoat which he left on a peg at the end of his eight-hour shift. When conversation turned to the recent closure of the pit, one man asked: 'I wonder what happened to Sonny's coat?'

To which Budgie replied: 'It'll still be there won't it? Where he left it hanging, on its peg.'

That image has stayed with me, Sonny the beautiful singer's overcoat hanging on its peg in the silent pitch black tunnel.

Arriving home, I put the pine cone on the bookshelf; wrapped the two oak wheels in an old blanket to return into storage until we moved to Hove. Jackie and I decided to offer one wheel to a museum and have the other one mounted in a glass case there.

The pine cone from the tree that marks the site of Hoyland Common's first mine will also find a place on a bookshelf.

27.

THE REFERENDUM ON WHETHER TO leave or remain in the European Union was held on 23 June 2016. Jackie had travelled up from Hove. We both voted remain and pushed our voting slips into black ballot boxes in the Methodist Chapel over our garden wall where swifts squealed overhead or swooped up to their nests in the chapel eaves.

We stayed up late to watch television; early results suggested remain might win. Our constituency, Sheffield Hallam, and Hove voted remain. But, as dawn broke, leave campaign supporters were on television cheering, laughing, waving their arms in the air and hoisting people on to each other's shoulders.

A few weeks earlier when Jackie and I were walking to the railway station in Sheffield city centre to renew our rail cards, we saw a small group of people. A young black man sat on a bench leaning forward, arms dangling by his side, dreadlocks covering his face. Three or four young Asian women in hijabs were talking to a man we couldn't see, but he sounded agitated and aggressive. Moments later, the young man sat up, threw his arms up in the air and shouted, 'I don't even want to be here', in despair, before flopping back to his earlier position, dreadlocks again covering his face. The man he'd been addressing, whose face I hadn't been able to see, walked off cockily, arms swinging by his side. He must have been telling the lad to 'get back to his own country'.

When we walked back from the station he was still there, this young man, being comforted by two of the women in hijabs. I tried to speak to him myself, but he didn't look up.

The day before the referendum Jackie and I walked down to Endcliffe Park. A warm sunny day, swallows hunting insects flew low over the grassy area in front of the children's playground and café. We sat on a bench, watching parents pushing their children on swings, helping them up slides. There were European accents and languages among them ... Polish ... French ... German ... spoken by people who had come to the UK to work and settled with their families. Three mothers in hijabs with broad Sheffield accents laughed with their children. A fellow we knew with a Caribbean accent went past, walking his recently acquired retired racing greyhound on a lead. 'Is he used to living in a house yet,' we asked, 'after years of living in kennels?' What anxieties would these people be feeling as Brexit votes were cast? As dawn broke on the outcome, it can only have confirmed what experience had probably already taught them. They were no longer welcome.

On the day of the referendum I saw Melanie, a recent science graduate from Sheffield University, shelf-stacking in Sainsbury's. I'd often chatted with her when I bought groceries and lately the topic had been Brexit. Along with all the young workers in the supermarket, she was going to vote remain; the only one who wasn't was an older man who owned his own house. Melanie had helped push the large wire cages full of groceries, fresh fruit and flowers unloaded from lorries from Europe every few days, timed to arrive just in time to keep the supermarket constantly stocked with fresh goods. She feared leaving the largest trading block in the world, with which we had such interconnected ties, would plunge us into an uncertain future. She'd thought her parents had come round to her way of thinking until ringing them earlier to see what they thought about the result, she was angry when they told her how, worried about immigration, they'd voted to leave. Throughout the country, many young people shared her anger.

When I rang Katie in Hove, she and her friends also felt let down by the over-sixties. It was alright for their generation, they fumed. They'd had the opportunity of free college and university education, trade unions, apprenticeships, good wages; bought their homes and been entitled to good state pensions, drawn at a reasonable age. Yet their generation, *my* generation, didn't seem to care that by voting to leave the European Union, more likely than not, they would have made their children's and grand-children's futures both economically and culturally poorer.

Many people claimed to have voted leave because they were concerned high levels of immigration would put even more strain on already over-stretched local services, such as housing, schools, GP surgeries and hospitals. As well as fearing that there would be fewer jobs available for themselves and their children, they were worried about lower wages because immigrants from poorer countries were cheaper to employ, angry perhaps at losing their self-respect and sense of identity, abandoned by politicians over the years. However, I would guess that some leave voters would have been as disgusted as Jackie and I were if, the morning after the result, they had read in the newspaper, as we had, how Polish families in Cambridgeshire had cards posted through their letterboxes saying 'No more Polish scum' and how, in one town, a Polish shop had been burnt to the ground.

I wonder how Polish families who settled here generations ago felt. Polish pilots played an important part in defeating the German Luftwaffe in the Battle of Britain, after all, having honed their skill in the skies over Europe before joining the Royal Air Force. Polish men came to work in the mines after the war and settled in Hoyland Common, workmates of my dad. One, nick-named Joe Pole, was buried in a roof fall at Rockingham Colliery and when my dad and other colleagues dug him out they thought he was okay until they discovered his foot was hanging off. As a young man, I used to talk to a Pole I knew in the Star pub at the top of Tinker Lane and enjoyed listening to his war experiences and about his life in Poland. A lovely Polish family lived in a prefab opposite us in Hoyland Common. Polish families were part of our community, our neighbours and friends.

One morning before the referendum vote, as I queued in the bank, I got into a conversation with a woman who told me she worked for a company which looked into suspected fraud cases and that she was only in Sheffield for the day. Then, out of the blue, she told me how furious she'd been when her son came back from primary school one day and said his teacher had taught the whole class how to say 'good morning' in Polish.

Before she retired in 2008, Jackie taught at Sharrow Primary School, about a mile away from where we live. She loved working there, teaching girls and boys of many nationalities; white British, second-generation Pakistani, children whose parents had moved here from India, Africa, Afghanistan and other countries, as well as Eastern Europe. Aleksander, a six year old in Jackie's class, was from Poland. He was a fun-loving lad who, after having a pot put on a broken leg, loved being raced around the playground in a wheelchair by his friends, pot raised in the air. His father thanked Jackie for teaching him English. But she hadn't; he'd picked it up himself by listening to her and the other children in the class.

Łukasz, another six-year-old, had come to Sheffield with his parents from a rural area in their homeland. A painfully shy lad, he spent his first days under a table and wouldn't come out. Until one morning from his hiding place he spotted a toy tractor on a classroom shelf and pointed to it. Jackie took it down and held it just in front of him, luring him out. When he took it she said 'tractor'. He repeated 'tractor'. His first word in English.

Who could have imagined that, in June 2016, families who'd lived here for generations or arrived more recently, like Łukasz and Aleksander's, would be made to feel so unwelcome?

28.

TODAY, IN SHEFFIELD, LOOKING THROUGH the bedroom drawers for items related to her family history, Jackie came across something that had belonged to her maternal Grandma: a small cream linen bag with a scalloped edge and three beautifully embroidered green clover leaves. I hadn't seen it before and when she opened the bag I thought she'd taken out a folded piece of lace before she separated it into two pieces. Enjoying keeping me guessing, she held up the end of one, what looked like a narrow knee-length stocking. Only then did she gently put her hand inside the delicate length of lace and pull it up her arm to her elbow. It was one of the pair of cream lace gloves her grandma had worn at her wedding.

The details of Jackie's grandparents' marriage are written in spidery black ink on her marriage certificate, which we also have on the table before us. They married on 2 December 1903, a ceremony 'solemnized at the Parish Church in the Parish of Gringley on the Hill in the County of Nottinghamshire.' Her grandma's maiden name was Beatrice Anderson and she was 22 years old when she married Frederick Richardson, Jackie's then 33-year-old grandad, rank or profession: 'Carter'.

Around the time their daughter Dorothy, Jackie's mother, was born in 1916 they had left Nottinghamshire and Jackie's grandad became a tenant farmer on the Fitzwilliam Wentworth Estate. He kept two shire horses, a large and strong breed with a gentle nature. We have a photograph of one; glistening black, it has a white forehead and white 'feathering' above its hooves. When her mother was older, she lived into her nineties, she would tell us about life on the farm each weekend when we took her for a walk around the village.

On her birthday and at Christmas we took her for a meal in a restaurant in Wentworth. As a girl in the 1920s, this low one-storey stone building had been the blacksmith's shop. We never tired of listening to her stories of her dad's expert horsemanship. She told us how when one of their shire horses needed shoeing he would occasionally let her hold its reins herself as they walked there together. She remembered pumping bellows, red hot coals, red hot metal hammered into shape on the anvil, the blacksmith holding the horse's hoof between his knees to fit the shoe, smoke and the smell of burning, and the nails hammered in. And how throughout all this, the horse stood calmly, unbothered, proving what her dad had told her was true: horses' hooves are made of the same stuff as our fingernails and painless. Her dad never rode a horse until it had been shod, but after it had, he'd lead it out and stand on a low stone wall just outside the blacksmith's to mount it, then reach down to pull up his seven-year-old daughter Dorothy to sit behind him. They would then ride bareback together along Coaley Lane and into the farmyard, where her dad would dismount and then lift her down.

She told us how her mother, Jackie's grandmother, would pack a wicker basket with bread and cheese, along with a ceramic flagon of ale, for her to take to her dad in the fields. In spring, she'd see him walking behind the horse, holding and guiding the plough it was pulling as it turned the earth into long furrows. At harvest time, a horse-drawn 'grain binding machine' cut the corn, separated the grain and bundled the straw into sheaves. And when she carried her basket into the field she'd see her dad sitting on what looked like a tractor seat on the grain binder, as it was pulled through the golden crop. Whether he was ploughing or harvesting, when he spotted her entering the field carrying the wicker basket he would call, 'Whoa', and halt the horses.

Jackie's grandad bought his ale from a horse-drawn cart that delivered to the farms on the Fitzwilliam Estate. Their farm was a mile or so outside Wentworth village. And rather than walk, as she did most school days, on the delivery day to their farm her mother cadged a lift and climbed up among the barrels of ale. Arriving in the village she would jump off the cart and run to the stone-built elementary school next to the church on Back Lane.

It was raining the day Jackie's mother, aged eleven, with holes in the soles of her shoes and her feet soaking wet, sat the exam for grammar school. She passed, but her parents couldn't afford to pay for the uniform. We have a photograph of Jackie's grandad Richardson in a field with his legs stretched out before him. His hair is neatly combed and he has a bushy moustache. Dressed as if he has just returned from church, he is wearing a dark suit and waistcoat, white shirt and tightly-knotted tie. Jackie's mother told us that often, as her parents, herself, four sisters and two brothers sat around their scrubbed wooden farmhouse table at breakfast, their dad would say the Richardson family had been well-off until an uncle emigrated to Australia taking the family fortune with him. He'd search the newspaper hoping to see a notice of a will in which some of the lost family money had been left to him.

Jackie's mother, Dorothy, liked to read the paper too, but as soon as she opened it her mother would tap her hand and tell her to stop reading. Reading newspapers was for men. Not girls.

It was around this time that the Richardsons left Wentworth and moved to another farm on the Wentworth Estate in Upper Hoyland. Bill, the oldest boy, who won prizes for the straightness of his furrows in ploughing competitions, worked on the farm, as did his younger brother George. The three older sisters, Edith, Elsie and Alice, had left home and worked in service. Her sister Mary, who was four years younger, still went to school. Being the older of the two, Jackie's mother helped out on the farm. When their udders were heavy with milk, she brought the mooing cows in from the fields. Then, sat on a wooden three-legged stool in the milking parlour, she held the cow's full teat between her first finger and thumb and used her other fingers to squirt warm milk into a shiny metal bucket. And occasionally into her mouth. And so it went on, time after time after time: Finger and thumb, other three fingers squeeze. Finger and thumb, other three fingers squeeze. On weekends and school holidays she did a milk round with her brother George, who drove the cart. When they pulled up outside a cottage, Jackie's mother climbed up on to the back among the metal churns, took the jug handed up to her by the cottage's resident and dipped her ladle into an open churn before filling it with milk.

She and George were good pals, whooping with joy as they rode down the fields on a homemade go-kart. Sometimes he gave her a ride down the lane on his bike, him standing up on the pedals and her on the saddle. We have a photo of them in a field with that bike. George, seventeen or eighteen, has brushed-back hair and is in a dark suit, white shirt and dark tie, holding the handlebars and saddle. Jackie's mother, fourteen or fifteen, stands beside him, with her hand on his shoulder. Her hair is swept to one side just above her right eye and she is wearing a cardigan over a short white dress, black stockings and laced shoes. They look like a happy brother and sister from a prosperous family. But within a year or two of it being taken their dad died.

Also on our table is a carbon copy of a hand-written receipt from Hoyland Council which itemises the details and cost of Jackie's grandad's burial in Kirk Balk Cemetery. 'Name of deceased: Frederick Richardson. Age: 64. Date of death: 4th November 1932. Day of internment: 8th November at 3.30pm.

Mode of internment: Earthen Grave. The costs of the burial are then set out in three columns; pounds, shillings and pence:

	£	s	d
Purchase of Grave	3	-	-
Internment Fee	1	5	-
Certificate, including stamp	-	3	-
Minister's Fee	-	5	-
Total	4	13	-

We have the certificate, including the stamp of Hoyland Urban District Council, granting the exclusive right of burial in the grave space at the cemetery situated at Kirk Balk, and confirming three pounds was paid for the purchase by Beatrice Richardson, 122 Upper Hoyland, in the County of Yorks. Poor grieving Beatrice had the right to bury her husband there, but as a widow she didn't have the right to continue living on a farm they rented from the Wentworth Estate. Her worries of what would become of her if she lost her home at the age of fifty-three were, however, lifted when nineteen-year-old son George took over the tenancy.

We have a couple of photos of Jackie's grandma in which her hair is worn in a short bob. In one of them she looks pensive, dressed in a black pinafore dress, a white blouse, white stockings and shoes with a strap as she scatters seed for the hens in the farmyard. In the other, wearing a striped dress, she sits in the grass in a field, smiling faintly as she looks at Fly the sheepdog by her side. She looks around fifty and these could have been the last photographs taken of her as a farmer's wife. A year or so later George married and gave up the farm. And Jackie's grandma was then forced to leave the life she had lived for twenty-nine years.

Bill, the eldest, had left farming. Her older sisters, Edith, Elsie and Alice, were in service. Jackie's mother was about to go into service in Bradford and younger sister Mary had gone to live with an uncle. Jackie's mother was the only one there to see *her* mother leave, and told us that, although she couldn't be sure, she thought she must have been crying because when she walked up the hill and away from the farm she didn't glance back once.

The stone ivy-covered farmhouse, 122 Upper Hoyland, was the last home she could call her own. The rest of her life was spent living in other people's houses. She moved to Worksop to live with her brother, Walter, and worked as a housekeeper for families elsewhere. Then, after she retired, each of her four married daughters took their turn to provide her with a home.

She moved into Calvert Street in 1957. Jackie was ten years old and remembers Grandma Richardson's severe-looking round wire National Health glasses and how, when watching *Sunday Night at the London Palladium* on television, her grandma was shocked and disgusted when the dancing girls moved aside the large feather fans they were holding and kicked their legs.

Jackie shared her small bedroom with her grandma. There wasn't room for a dressing table, but a space was cleared on a chest of drawers for grandma's brush, comb, hand mirror, her small purple bottle of 'Evening in Paris' perfume and her 'Lily of the Valley' talcum powder and soap, both of them bought from Woolworths in Barnsley. It was a tight squeeze fitting in two single beds, but it was cheerful with its white and blue dotted wallpaper and blue and yellow woodwork, and there was enough room between the beds to fit in a chair for grandma to sit on while Jackie did her hair. She remembers the lovely smell of her perfume, and dampening her soft silvery hair into waves and holding them in place with the teeth of metal hair grips.

Jackie's dearest memory of her grandma is on dark winter evenings when they sat together in the firelight, her grandma gently rocking in the rocking chair and Jackie sitting on the rug bedside her, as her mother played sweet sad tunes on her mouth organ and they both quietly sang along:

The falling leaves drift by the window...
The autumn leaves of red and gold...

One night, Jackie's dad lifted her out of bed and put her in her parent's bed to sleep. Next morning, her mother told her Grandma had died.

I'm looking at the death certificate with Jackie. Under various typed headings, hand written in ink, it says Beatrice Richardson, aged 76, was the widow of Frederick Richardson a farm horseman, and that she died on 9 March 1959 at 17 Calvert Street, Hoyland Common. Cause of death, a coronary thrombosis, a heart attack, diagnosed and signed-off by Dr M. Allot.

Seeing Doctor Marie's name on the death certificate helped Jackie piece together what probably happened. Her mum and dad would have been alerted by her grandma calling out in the night, or maybe one of them had gone into the bedroom to check she was alright. Jackie's mother would then have hurried across Calvert Street and through Doctor Eric and Marie Allott's garden gate and knocked on their door. When Jackie was ill in the night it was always Doctor Eric who came. That night it was Marie. Trying to imagine it, we wondered if she put her black doctor's bag on the chest of drawers bedside Grandma Richardson's hand mirror, brush and comb, her small purple bottle of 'Evening in Paris' perfume and her 'Lily of the Valley' talc and soap.

She too was buried in Kirk Balk Cemetery, in the same grave as her husband Fredrick, and in the funeral service held in St Peter's Church before the burial Jackie gently placed a small bunch of violets on her grandma's coffin.

When we go to Hove, Jackie will find a place in our bedroom drawers for the cream linen bag with three embroidered clover leaves, containing the lace gloves her grandma wore at her wedding.

Two

Jackie's mother, Dorothy, with her brother George

29.

EVERY SATURDAY AFTERNOON, JACKIE AND I would drive over to Hoyland and take her mother, Dorothy, on a walk around her birthplace, Wentworth village. When the photo we are looking at now was taken, daffodils were in bloom in the grass beside the path. A handsome grey-haired ninety-year-old, she is dressed in a pale green coat stands between Jackie and our daughter Katie, the church spire reaching high into the sky behind them. In another photograph, taken on the same day in the same spot by Jackie, I am standing with her mother and Katie.

In the autumn of that year when the nights were drawing in, we discovered a flock of starlings roosted for the night in a holly bush. As we approached it the flock fell silent. Then, when we had walked a few paces past, their incessant chattering started up again. Jackie's mother said that over the years she had seen the number of starlings decline, going on to tell us how she had once walked out of Low Wood with her sister, Alice, and large flocks of them darkened the sky and descended on the fields, turning them black as far as the eye could see.

That afternoon was probably the last time Jackie and I walked around Wentworth arm-in-arm with her mother. From then onwards I pushed her in a wheelchair while Jackie walked beside her. Social Services had provided her with an alarm with a cord to wear around her neck. After suffering a heart attack she fell on the alarm, and by chance, her arm or another part of part of her body, activated it as an ambulance was passing her house and alerted the crew, who stretchered her out of the house and drove her to Barnsley hospital, sirens blaring. When we arrived she lay in bed connected up to tubes. A nurse took us to one side and told us Jackie's mother didn't have long to live. But we hadn't been sitting at her bedside long when, to our amazement, we saw her blood pressure rise to normal on one of the monitors.

When a young male doctor arrived, he smiled, told her she'd made a remarkable recovery, then tentatively asked if she would like to sign a 'Do Not Resuscitate' form, so the doctors would know what to do if she had another attack and wasn't so lucky next time. She didn't understand. Before the doctor could explain I chipped in and said, 'He's asking if next time your heart stops, do you want resurrecting?' The wrong word had slipped out of my mouth. Laughing, the doctor said, 'I'm afraid we can't promise that, only God could do that.' Jackie then asked her mum if her heart did stop, would she like them to try and get it beating again? Knowing how spirited she was, her answer didn't come as a surprise. Without hesitation she said, 'If there is a chance of that – yes.'

Within a week or two, Jackie's mother was back home in Kirk Balk. But a few weeks later she had another fall at home and was back in Barnsley General with a broken hip. The doctors pieced it back together with a large screw – we saw the X-ray hooked over the rail at the bottom of her bed.

She was then moved from hospital to Mount Vernon, a Barnsley convalescent home where physiotherapists helped her to walk again using a tubular steel walking frame. The single beds she'd bought for our kids, John and Katie, to sleep in when they stayed with their grandma were still in the spare room, and on the morning she was coming home we drove over and set up one for her downstairs in the small dining room.

Dorothy hadn't seen her home for many weeks and when she came in with two women occupational therapists we watched as, using her frame, she shuffled across the living room, lowered herself into her favourite armchair and was so relieved to be back she cried. The therapists needed to check that she could manage by herself once her carer's had left, so they set her the task of making a cup of tea. She filled the electric kettle with water from the tap in the kitchen sink, but as she reached to plug it in, she overbalanced and fell, her steel frame crashing to the floor beside her. It was heartbreaking to see Jackie's mother lying there, her hopes that she would be able to return home immediately gone.

She was of the generation of poor rural farmers who seemed to just get on with it when faced with adversity. As a child, she had often sat at her desk in Wentworth Church School with soaking wet feet because she had holes in the soles of her shoes and her parents couldn't afford to buy a new pair. She'd had her infected tonsils removed without anaesthetic on the scrubbed farmhouse kitchen table. So, although leaving her Kirk Balk home of over sixty years must have been very upsetting, she didn't show it and adjusted to life as a resident in Hoyland Royal Court Care Home.

We arranged for her room to overlook Beacon Fields, as we'd done with my stepdad, Bob. Poor old Bob no longer remembered his connection to his beloved Wentworth, whereas Dorothy loved gazing at the fields where her dad had walked behind his black gentle shire horse, holding, pulling and guiding the plough as it turned the earth into long straight furrows.

One afternoon, while I was doing tutorials with a group of students at Sheffield Hallam University's Psalter Lane site, a work colleague knocked on the lecture room door, entered, and was followed in by Jackie. She told me the care home had rung and said that her mother had been taken ill and was in an ambulance on her way to hospital. As we drove to Barnsley I reminded Jackie of the last time her mother was rushed in with a heart attack. We had watched her blood pressure rise to normal, hadn't we, and the same could happen today. But when we arrived we weren't taken on to the ward, instead shown into a waiting room. On one wall was a pair of sliding wooden doors on which, in large black letters, was written 'DO NOT OPEN'. After a while, fed up of waiting, I told Jackie I was going to open them and see what is in there. 'Don't,' she said, just as a surgeon, still in his V-necked operating theatre clothes, came in and gently explained to Jackie they had done their best but hadn't been able to save her mum. Then, sliding open the wooden doors, he said, 'She's in here.' What an awful unexpected shock it was to see her on a bed in a hospital gown, eyes closed, so lifeless. Her heart, which had beat every second for ninety-one years, was now stilled.

Our son, John, and Katie came up from Brighton on the train to their beloved grandma Dot's funeral service. Jackie's cousin Paul and his wife, Karen, drove over from Lincolnshire. Other relatives and friends filled almost half the pews of St Peter's Church. And although that's where she had wanted the service to be, rather than being buried in Kirk Balk Cemetery like her mother and father, she had asked to be cremated and have her ashes scattered in Wentworth.

Today, after putting away the photographs, Jackie seeks out the urn holding her mum's ashes and, on this late September day with fair weather clouds sailing across a bright blue sky, we drive over to Wentworth to carry out her mother's wishes.

The stubble fields around the village are interspersed with freshly-cut rectangular bails of golden straw. After parking, we walk up Clayfields Lane and look across the steeply rising fields at a row of trees stretching across the horizon on Beacon Hill, before continuing along Coaley Lane where the fields have been ploughed. Where the earth has peeled off the plough blade, the furrows are smooth and have the dull silver colour of medieval armour. In the sky above a lone twittering swallow dive bombs a hovering kestrel. Walking on, we turn on to the path that leads to Beacon Hill trees. The first is a dead sycamore, the next few hawthorn trees covered in deep red berries, then the sycamore that Jackie has decided will be the tree under which she spreads her mother's ashes.

The is on the edge of a field where, as a girl, Jackie's mother had carried a basket of sandwiches and a flagon of beer for her dad's lunch at harvest time. The same field now is ready for the planting of next year's crops and I can smell recently-turned earth as Jackie scatters handfuls from the urn and then, with tears in her eyes, and in her sweet beautiful voice, sings her mother's favourite hymn:

> We plough the fields and scatter
> The good seed on the land
> But it is fed and watered by God's almighty hand
> He sends the snow in winter
> The warmth to swell the grain
> The breezes and the sunshine
> And soft refreshing rain
>
> All good gifts around us
> Are sent from heaven above,
> Then thank the Lord
> O thank the Lord
> For all his love.

After she has spread the ashes, we walk back to the village and call in the Rockingham Arms. I buy a couple of drinks at the bar, non-alcoholic beer for me, apple juice for Jackie, and carry them over to the same table we sat at when on our first date in October 1965. We had loved walking the couple of miles or so to this country pub with its stone-flagged floor to sit near the open fire,

Jackie with a half-pint, me a pint, chatting and tucking into roast beef sandwiches. In later years, on warm summer evenings we used to push John and Katie to the Rockingham Arms in their double buggy to sit in the pub garden with its bowling green and magnificent copper beech tree. We have fond associations with the 'Rock' that stretch back fifty years.

We don't want to completely cut our ties with home, and plan to come up once or twice a year to visit family, friends and favourite places, but we haven't yet decided where to stay. In a soulless modern hotel in Sheffield city centre? A cottage on the Chatsworth Estate, to which we had no connection? As we sit in the Rockingham Arms, I realise it will make our occasional trips up north more enjoyable if we stay here, bed and breakfast, in the pub. Jackie agrees. From here, all our special places and the people dear to us will be but a short drive away; all our Hines relatives in Sheffield, neighbours and friends there, our cousins in Hoyland Common, and lifelong friends in our pit village. We leave the pub discussing the best months to come north, maybe in spring when the curlew sings its sad burbling song on the moor, or perhaps autumn, when the moor is purple with heather.

I propose visiting our old haunts in spring, when the field in front of Tankersley Old Hall is yellow with buttercups. We could sit on the bench opposite the ruins and watch to see if the kestrels are nesting yet. Then something totally unexpected happens. It's as if an alarm bell simultaneously rings in both of our heads. We look at each other, startled. In that momentary gaze, unspoken doubts about living in Hove seem to surface as if we have realised the enormity of our decision to leave our homes of seventy years, the histories of our lives and landscapes that shaped who we are.

We know now that we don't want to live on the Sussex coast; we want to stay in Sheffield. And yet, the more we think about the emotional and financial investment that has already gone into the flat we nevertheless change our minds again and decide that going to Hove must be the right thing to do. Until, one morning in Sheffield railway station, we are again overcome by doubt. Jackie is going to stay in our flat for a few weeks while I stay home and I'm at the station to see her off. I'm not sure why, maybe they are changing the timetables, but no return tickets are on sale for the journey, just singles. Jackie buys her ticket and then, instead of putting it into her purse, shows it to me. Along with details of travel and price, there are orange stripes at the top and bottom. To the left of the ticket it reads:

SNR

From

SHEFFIELD

To

BRIGHTON

Then in the bottom right hand corner is printed:

SINGLE

Those six words carry such significance. SNR, both of us in our seventies. The direction of the journey. The stark severe word SINGLE. Suddenly and unexpectedly, it is brought home to us that we will soon be on a one-way journey.

On the platform, as we sit on a bench drinking from paper cups with announcements of arrivals, departures and delays on a tannoy overhead, we have to remind ourselves of how after our granddaughter was born we wanted to go south to be nearer our family and play a part in Emily's life. Just as our parents had been present in the lives of our children, Katie and John.

30.

I TRAVELLED FROM SHEFFIELD TO join Jackie in our flat for a week at the end of May 2016. Later in the summer, I was there for three weeks from the end of July into August, then for a couple of weeks in October and early November. I loved being together as a family with our Katie, Dan and two-year-old Emily in the flat next door, our son John only a twenty-minute walk away from Hove, soon to be our new home.

One day, Jackie and I walked along the seafront when the tide was out. We were surprised to see gulls flying high above the promenade holding shellfish in their beaks, before dropping them and then swooping down to eat the limpets or dog whelks from their broken shells on the road.

When Katie rang from next door to say they were on their way, I loved to open the door and see Emily with her lovely dark brown eyes and brown shoulder-length hair smiling up at us from her pushchair. Most mornings, we walked to the bottom of the road, lifted Emily up to press the button on the crossing and walked along the seafront, pausing to point out surfboarders as they hung on to brightly-coloured kites skimming across the sea, before choc ices under an umbrella outside Mrs Bumble's Café.

To go shopping, we walked up past the row of elms, crossed tree-lined New Church Road and on to Richardson Road. At the bread shop, we bought fresh baked bread, scones and delicious mince pies. The greengrocer sold locally produced fruit and veg, fresh eggs and his own homemade pies; we got our papers from the newsagent. When John came over, Katie joined us in the café for afternoon tea, Emily sipping her baby chino through a straw.

Before the sofa arrived, we sat on dark grey bean bags on the polished floorboards. The large cardboard box they came in was still in the spare bedroom. When Katie brought Emily around, I took it into the living room, turned it on its side and opened the flaps that had been the lid. It was lovely to see our granddaughter run across the room and crawl into what was now her playhouse.

In late October, Jackie and I came down to the flat to celebrate our forty-sixth wedding anniversary with our family. When John joined us, as Emily played, he and Katie sat on bean bags and we sat on the sofa, Jackie asked if they'd been in touch with their friends lately who'd moved away from Sheffield on leaving home.

John's friend, Matt – in fact best man at his wedding – was now a lecturer in Classics at a London university. John told us how, when he'd met up with him recently in the capital, they had visited Art Galleries together. Katie has a friend who had lived a couple of hundred yards up the road from us, friends since nursery school. Married, she has a daughter, lives in Nottingham, and works in a bookshop. It was harder now the two of them had children, Katie said, but they, along with another couple of school friends, still met up occasionally for a weekend in nice cities like Cambridge and Norwich.

Katie and John love Sheffield, came back on regular visits, but have now lived half their lives in Brighton and Hove and built up new groups with stories, memories and affection for a new home.

It was different for me.

I have lived in Sheffield since 1981. Most weekends Jackie and I drive for a few minutes towards the moor, park the car and walk the field paths of Whirlow Hall Farm. In spring, the barley fields are knee high; the field edges beside the stone walls a blue haze of wildflowers, blue forget-me-nots, purple vetch, tiny blue birdseye, speedwell. In one large meadow, we regularly see four or five mad March hares tearing after a single female they want to mate with until she, the jill, stops and uses her front paws to box her pursuers, keeping them at bay. In autumn, in late afternoon just before dusk, in a field of short-grazed grass, we have seen hundreds of rooks congregate in flocks of around fifty. To gain lift, the first flock turns into the west wind blowing in from the moor and, once airborne, then heads south to night roosts in Ecclesall Woods. After a minute or so, another flock takes flight, then another, and then another... an autumn ritual witnessed four and a half centuries ago by William Shakespeare: 'Light thickens and the crow makes wing to th' rooky wood.'

In spring, we drive a couple of miles up the road to walk on the moor and listen for the sad burbling song of the curlew, the haunting, forlorn call of the golden plover, and watch the black and white lapwings, which we call peewits, rising and tumbling in the sky calling *pee-wit ... pee-wit*.

Born in Hoyland Common in 1945, I spent the first half of my life in a village where every street, field and wood carries so many memories; squealing swifts flying over streets and up to nests under the eaves of terraced stone houses. High in the sky, larks singing over the meadows. Training my kestrels to the lure throughout summer, then, when the hedges and cobwebs glisten with dew and the robins sing their sweet sad song, releasing them back into the wild. The walks through the fields to Tankersley Church and the Old Hall to see if kestrels are nesting. The local history; common land where oxen ploughed the furrows; the discovery of the first coalmine; my family, friends, and the people in our village; my experience there has made me who I am.

I had loved spending every day with our family over the last couple of weeks, but thinking about Sheffield, and particularly about Hoyland Common, where the stories of my life and those who came before me have been told, made me realise that the pull is so strong that I will never feel at home in Hove.

These thoughts had been stirred up after the conversation with John and Katie, and I had been going over them in my head while strolling along Hove seafront.

It was late afternoon when I got back to the flat. The autumn light was streaming through the large bay window, throwing leaf patterns on its white walls from a tree outside. Jackie was on the sofa, turning up the hem on one of Emily's dresses. I sat beside her and said I needed to tell her what I'd been thinking about and my thoughts came pouring out: 'I'll never settle in Hove; we should never have rented the flat in the first place; I should have listened to you when you said we needed time to think about it, instead of rushing you into agreeing; telling you we need to offer six month's rent in advance and secure it now...'

'Calm down,' Jackie said, interrupting me in full flow. She told me that she too had been having doubts about moving down here permanently. She loved being with Katie and Emily but realised she couldn't rely on family and being a grandma for a fulfilling life. She needed to continue doing her art, but didn't think she would be able to by having the spare bedroom as a studio, as planned. The flat was lovely, but there wasn't enough natural light there and it was too small for everything she needed; her easel and brushes, a table for her paint pots. Nor was there room to store finished paintings and any canvases waiting to be primed. And even if she had been able to manage to paint there, she said, she wouldn't, going on to say how there are some magnificent paintings of seascapes by such artists as Maggi Hambling, which catch the power and movement of the sea, but painting seascapes wasn't for Jackie. She needed to be in her studio in Sheffield.

I understood. Her portrait of Sonia Garcia Lorus, a student we knew, in which the yellow, green and red in her hairband matched the same three colours on the cover of the chair she was sitting in, won her first prize in the South Yorkshire Open, which was held in Barnsley Cooper Art Gallery, the place she'd passed on her first morning at art school, aged fifteen. Her portrait of Sally, our niece, whose striking blue eyes confidently hold the gaze of the person looking at the canvas, won first prize in the Derby Open. She has also had solo exhibitions of her work, such as the one at Piece Hall, Halifax, and had work shown in group exhibitions. One, *Reclaiming the Madonna: Artists as Mothers*, toured the country. We saw it in Lincoln's Usher Gallery.

As she sat on the sofa, needle in hand and Emily's dress on her lap, she told me how everything she had drawn and painted; portraits of relatives and friends: drawing and paintings of the natural world such as those of the hollow ancient oak trees in Chatsworth Park, a twenty-minute drive across the moors, have to come from her heart, have an emotional connection to home, and places dear to her. She reiterated how she needed to be in her studio, where she has worked for thirty-five years.

For Jackie, it wasn't just about her art, though. In Hove, she missed our walks around Tankersley and Wentworth, and out on the moor, only minutes away. What surprised me was the sudden unexpectedness of both our doubts – only days before, we had been so happy and relaxed down here with our family that we had paid the next six months' rent in advance.

Why hadn't we thought it through properly before I'd rushed us into renting the flat in the first place?

We ought to have realised that we would never feel truly settled away from our home patch, where we had spent all of our lives. We must have gone over it all for hours on that sofa until it got so dark we had to turn on the light. Later, in her diary, Jackie wrote: 'Couldn't sleep – too het up.'

Monday, a bright cold late autumn day, two days after we had made our decision to give up the tenancy. The surfboarders had been out in their wetsuits holding on to their kites as we walked along the seafront and we were now seated in the Bandstand Bar and Bistro, on Brighton beach. We had forgiven ourselves for rushing into rental, reasoning that had we missed an opportunity to live down here we would have constantly been on the lookout for another flat to rent. We had known Brighton and Hove for twenty years and had lovely times. So, it was understandable that we believed we could settle here happily. What we couldn't have anticipated and learnt, without the actual experience of renting the flat, was what a wrench it would be to leave our roots.

After Jackie finished her tea and me my caffè latte, we paid and walked back along the seafront, Jackie saying we could still enjoy coming down to the flat before the lease ran out in May. After that, we'd be able to go back to how it was before we rented it, both working at home and staying with Katie, Dan and Emily on visits. Grinning, I said, 'Let's see how much we could have saved if we'd done that instead,' calculating it as seven thousand five hundred pounds every six months for eighteen months in advance... that's just over twenty two thousand... then the cost of buying furniture.' It had taken a big chunk out of our savings, but we both agreed that we had loved having it.

Katie had kept Emily at home that day because she wasn't well, and Jackie rang to say we'd call in to see her. As we walked up the road, Katie was standing in the window with Emily in her arms, waving. Outside their flat as we waited for Katie to open the door and let us in, I couldn't help but be struck by the view. The leaves on the elm tree outside our place next door were turning golden; at the bottom of the road were the now familiar beach huts, red, blue and green, and beyond those the sea.

'This is such a lovely place to live,' I said. 'It's just that, for us, it isn't home.'

HOYLAND ROAD.

Hoyland Common, Hoyland Road, during the 1890s

Allott's Corner and Sheffield Road, focal points of the 1893 strike and on the route taken by thousands of locked-out miners in the year of the pit yard riot

Epilogue

31.

WE ARRIVED HOME IN SHEFFIELD on 6 May 2017, before the swifts. Driven by instinct and emotion, they would still be winging their way back. Rooks were cawing as I drove down the hill through the green tunnel of overhanging rookery trees.

After parking the car outside Tankersley Church, I crossed the road and walked down towards the Bullwood, where Margaret, my lifelong friend Budgie's wife, had told me their son Tom had spread some of his dad's ashes twelve years ago. To the right of the path, white cow parsley was growing next to a dry-stone wall covered in patches of lichen and green moss. Beyond the wall, a field of green winter wheat. The hedge on the left of the path had been 'layed', which is to say the branches at its base were cut half-way through, interwoven and left to grow into a green boundary hedge for the large house with stables beyond it. I remembered how one day I met Budgie as I carried stones up this path for our rockery. He'd pointed to the entangled branches of the hawthorn hedge and asked: 'Did tha notice it's been layed?' I hadn't.

Budgie was knowledgeable about the countryside and loved animals. Once, when we were in Miss Robinson's class in junior school, he heard that a boy with the unlikely nickname of Bleb, was selling a white mouse for one shilling and sixpence. Fired up by the idea of having a pet, he spent hours chopping firewood and then walking the streets knocking on doors trying to sell it. Eventually he raised the one shilling and sixpence and excitedly ran to Bleb's house to buy the mouse. It had been sold.

Next day, however, he used the money to buy another from a pet shop and, unknown to Miss Robinson, kept it in an Oxo tin in his desk. This was one of the only times Budgie seemed really happy at school apart from those fine days when she took us on a nature walk around Tankersley. In spring to observe a pond, its water heavy with frog spawn, say. Or in autumn to collect items for the nature table: red and gold leaves; conkers; beechnuts and sweet chestnuts. More often he seemed bored and started to mess about, ending up in the 'C' form when we moved to Kirk Balk Secondary Modern. I'd been encouraged by headmaster Ben to take an exam for Barnsley Tech, where I took 'O' levels, before going on to grammar school and Leicester's teacher-training college to study Environmental Science and develop a lifelong interest in biology, particularly evolution, and also in physics.

Often when Budgie and I had a pint together we'd laugh and talk with others. But sometimes when we sat on our own I'd tell him things about nature I found fascinating. Once, after a blood test, I told him how I'd stared in wonder at the small tube of red liquid that had been drained from my arm. Marvelling at the fact the iron atoms in that very blood had been blasted out of a dying star billions of years ago and had ended up pumping around my body. He told me he found stuff like that 'dead interesting'.

While he was terminally ill, I reminded him of our earlier conversations about atoms created nearly fourteen billion years ago at the beginning of the universe becoming part of us. Of how, when we died, our ashes would be recycled in the surrounding soil and plants. I can't be sure of course, but as he lay on that sofa reflecting on what I'd said, I sensed that my friend liked the idea of being part of this eternal life cycle.

A great spotted woodpecker hammered its beak on a tree somewhere to the left in the Bullwood. I walked on past a line of saplings beside the path, then stopped. This clearing in the wood, with its magnificent oak and beech trees coming into leaf, is where Budgie's son, Tom, would have scattered his father's ashes. Among autumn's fallen leaves, purple violets, pink purslane and red campions in flower, bluebells have again bloomed in a purple-blue haze. It is here, in one of his favourite spots, that the calcium and phosphorous in Budgie's bones would indeed have released their nutrients into the soil, flowers and trees, with the result that his atoms were now part of this beautiful place.

I walked back up the path and opened the lychgate into the churchyard, where pale yellow primroses now covered the grass between the grave stones. For a while I sat on the wooden bench beside the church, as I had with Jackie in the autumn of 1965, when we had first walked together across the fields to Tankersley.

After paying my respects at my stepdad Bob's grave, I stood beside the one belonging to my brother, Barry.

And then, beyond our village of Hoyland Common, on the horizon, I looked towards the spire of St Peter's where our mother and dad are buried in Kirk Balk Cemetery, next to the church.

32.

THE WEATHER WAS OVERCAST. For three days we didn't see a single solitary swift. Wednesday 10 May was bright and sunny and we were in the kitchen with the door open when we heard them arrive and hurried into the garden.

Six or seven flew fast and low over our heads, squealing. Two or three of these flew up and clung to the chapel wall beneath the nest holes for a few seconds, then, in a head-first dive, they seemed to be about to crash into the ground before curving up again to re-join the fast-flying group of those overhead. Other swifts had climbed higher, their flights alternating between bursts of flickering wings and glides; their arced wings and streamlined bodies black against the bluest sky.

It was hotter on Saturday 17 June when Katie, Dan and Emily travelled up by train to stay with us. One day, we all walked down to Endcliffe Park café and had lunch together, surrounded by families of grandparents, parents and children at other tables. From a children's menu, chalked on a blackboard, Dan ordered pasta for Emily which she ate with a spoon. Later, as she enjoyed an ice cream, Jackie and I looked at each other and smiled.

Three months later in the warmth of August, towards the end

of the day, white fair weather clouds sailed slowly across the sky and the moor was purple with heather, Jackie and I carrying out what had become a yearly ritual: me cutting those few sprigs of heather for her to put in a small green silk bag and post to Katie and Dan, wishing them good luck for the year ahead on their fifth wedding anniversary, along with the card and presents for Emily's third birthday.

And as always up here on the moor, we gazed at the horizon.

Richard with David Bradley during the making of *Kes*

ABOUT THE AUTHOR

RICHARD HINES, the son of a miner, was born and raised in Hoyland Common, a pit village on the Fitzwilliam Wentworth Estate in South Yorkshire. He has worked as a building labourer, in an office, as a falcon trainer on the Ken Loach film *Kes*, and has been a deputy headmaster. Later, he became a documentary filmmaker and production company founder, making films that gave a voice to working class women and men for Channel 4 and the BBC, and also lecturered at Sheffield Hallam University. As a boy, he failed the entrance exam for grammar school and took refuge in nature, before one day happening upon a nest of kestrels in the ruins of a 16th-century hall. Captivated, he then trained one, which he called Kes. His experiences thereafter inspired his older brother, Barry, to write the novel *A Kestrel for a Knave*, which became the basis for Loach's film. Richard's previous book, the critically-acclaimed *No Way But Gentlenesse – A Memoir of How Kes, My Kestrel, Changed My Life*, was published by Bloomsbury in 2016. He lives in Sheffield and frequently walks on the nearby moors.

A GALLERY OF JACKIE'S ART

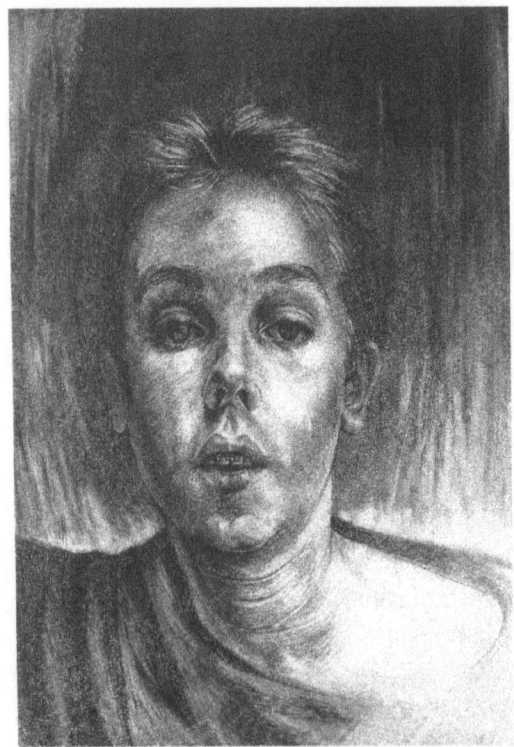

Adolescent Boy –
a portrait of Jackie
and Richard's son,
John Hines

Self-portrait,
exhibited in
touring exhibition
*Reclaiming the
Madonna - artists
as mothers.*

Ruth – another portrait exhibited in an exhibition

Sally and Sam – Exhibited at Halifax Piece Hall Art Gallery and other Galleries

Sally – an exhibited portrait by Jackie Hines.

WHAT PEOPLE HAVE SAID ABOUT
THE PLACE THAT KNOWS ME

RICHARD HINES had a fascinating story to tell in *No Way But Gentlenesse – A Memoir of How Kes, My Kestrel, Changed My Life*. The title of his second memoir, *The Place That Knows Me*, is taken from a quotation by John Clare: 'I have had some difficulties to leave the woods & heaths & and favourite spots that have known me so long.' Richard and his wife, Jackie, decided to move from their home in Yorkshire to Hove, on the south coast, where their daughter, son-in-law and infant granddaughter live, as well as their son. But in preparing to leave they experienced 'some difficulties' – related to their attachment to the landscape, community and history of the place where they were born and grew up.

The links between the past and present, between the individual, the family and the community, between the landscape and the people who live in it, and between human beings and other creatures – including birds, particularly swifts and horses working the land – are very strong. Class, education and employment are recurring issues. There's no sentimentality. Characters are brought to life by

Richard Hines's eye for detail, his ear for dialogue, and his dry sense of humour. There are flashes of anger, arising from childhood humiliations and personal experiences of class discrimination.

This memoir will speak to many readers, whether they have a similar sense of belonging or not. It touches on universal concerns, and shows how individual memories may illuminate a larger social history. There's a great deal of humour in the many anecdotes. Its use of local dialect is a delight. Many of its sentences have a pithy, poetic quality which touches the heart as well as the mind.

Alan Payne,
Published poet

AS A BOY, author Richard Hines captured and trained a kestrel, an act that awakened a love of wild nature which would transform his life. His elder brother, novelist Barry Hines, took Richard's story and turned it eventually into *Kes*, one of the great British films of the last century. In his first book, *No Way But Gentlenesse. No Way But Gentlenesse. A Memoir of How Kes, My Kestrel, Changed My Life*, Richard reclaimed his story.

In this new memoir, *The Place That Knows Me*, he recounts life in a northern mining village with all his customary grace and clarity. We hear the sound of clogs at dawn and the south Yorkshire dialect in its exotic otherness. Here are poverty, prejudice and the withholding of hope that defined the education system in the provisional north. Yet Hines also takes us to the open fields beyond ear-shot of the pit siren. Here are his places of flower meadows and birdsong. They create an alternative world to the caste system of industrial Britain and show us Hines's vanished childhood in all its wonderfully tender and lost complexity.

Mark Cocker
Award-winning author

Richard communicates his passion for the
landscape of his home town with great warmth.

Ken Loach

I enjoyed this memoir very much. It is very well
written, wholly authentic and an important record
of a fast vanishing past working-class history. The
personal story – of belonging and rediscovery – is
very engaging and well done.

Jeremy Mynot
Writer on the natural world

A vivid, moving, and important story
of working class history.

Conor Jameson
Writer and biographer

I love this book. It is beautiful, evocative,
elegiac and very moving.

Stephanie Cox
Writer and reviewer

*Rockingham colliery open day pamphlet – where Richard
and his friend, Budgie, read about the 1893 lockout and riot.*

Investigate our other titles and
stay up to date with all our latest releases at
www.scratchingshedpublishing.co.uk